Inhalt

Vorwort

Cool! richtet sich an Schüler/innen im Berufsvorbereitungsjahr sowie an Lernende in berufsvorbereitenden Kursen mit niedrigem Einstiegsniveau, z. B. Vorklasse / Berufsgrundbildungsjahr, BB10, Berufsfachschule oder außerschulische Einrichtungen.
Cool! entspricht den Richtlinien der verschiedenen Bundesländer.

Die Lehrwerksteile umfassen

- das einbändige Lehr- / Arbeitsbuch zum Reinschreiben
- als Sonderausgabe: das einbändige Lehr- / Arbeitsbuch mit Schüler-Software (Vokabeln, Grammatik, Hörverstehen)
- das Lehrerhandbuch mit Lehrer-Audio-CD (Lese- und Hörverständnistexte) und Lehrer-Service-CD-ROM.
  Das Handbuch enthält viele Unterrichtshilfen z. B. fotokopierbare Tests sowie Vorschläge zu Freiarbeitsmaterialien.

Aufbau des Lehr- / Arbeitsbuches

Die 12 klar strukturierten, kurzen Units sind nach dem Doppelseiten-Prinzip thematisch aufgebaut. Starter in jeder Unit ist die Motivations-Seite. Hier werden die im aktiven Wortschatz der Lernenden bereits vorhandenen englischen Ausdrücke auf motivierende Weise geübt.

Reading: Schwerpunkt Lesen
Ein längerer Lesetext wird ergänzt durch verschiedene Übungstypen, die sich zum größten Teil zunächst zur mündlichen Bearbeitung eignen.
Neue Vokabeln erscheinen *kursiv* im Text und im Vokabelkasten auf jeder Seite; der Grundwortschatz wird gefestigt und erweitert.

Grammar: Schwerpunkt Grammatik
Dieser Teil beinhaltet eine Strukturprogression in den 12 Units von leichteren zu schwierigeren grammatischen Inhalten.
Thematisch eingebettete Übungen unterschiedlicher Art dienen der Wiederholung und Festigung der Grammatikstrukturen.
Am Ende dieser Doppelseite steht eine Zusammenfassung des Grammatikschwerpunktes.

Listening: Schwerpunkt Hören
Für die gezielte Schulung des Hörverständnisses (HV) gibt es eine ◎ CD mit Texten und Dialogen aus den Units. Das Symbol kennzeichnet jeweils die Teile, zu denen Tonaufnahmen vorliegen. Die Hörverständnistexte sind im Anhang des Lehr- / Arbeitsbuches abgedruckt. Handlungs- und produktionsorientierte Aufgaben runden die Units ab.

Cool! bietet außerdem Übungen zum gelenkten und freien Sprechen und Schreiben.
Beispiele sind in blauer Schrift dargestellt (**Beispiel**).
Des Weiteren gibt es auf das Thema der Unit bezogene kurze Übersetzungen sowie Diktate.

Im Anhang finden Sie

- vier Prüfungsaufgaben mit den gängigsten Aufgabentypen
- den zugrunde gelegten Grundwortschatz
- die kapitelbegleitenden Wortlisten (englisch-deutsch) mit zusätzlichen Beispielsätzen, Synonymen / Gegensätzen, Wortfamilien, Definitionen
- die alphabetisch geordnete Wortschatzliste mit der Fundstelle im Lehr- / Arbeitsbuch
- alle Hörverständnistexte.

Auf dem Klappenumschlag finden Sie

- die wichtigsten unregelmäßigen Verben
- eine Übersicht der wichtigsten Grammatikstrukturen.

Der Schlüssel zu allen Übungen im Lehr- / Arbeitsbuch ist im Lehrerhandbuch zu Cool! abgedruckt.

Viel Spaß und Erfolg bei der Arbeit mit diesem Buch wünschen Ihnen

Autorinnen, Autoren und Redaktion

At home 1

A **Lots of words in German are the same in English. The pictures below show things you can find around your house. Write the names of each object below the picture.**
Schreiben Sie die Bezeichnungen für die Gegenstände unter die Bilder.

1. glass ____________

2. ____________

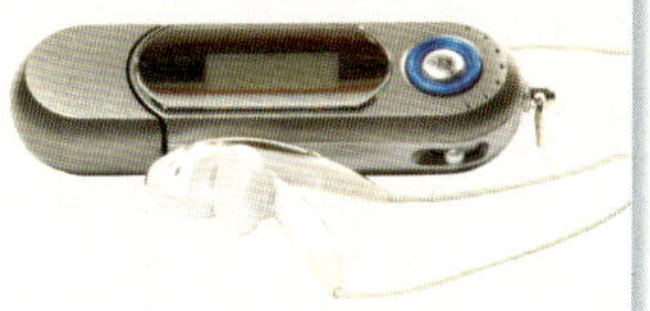

3. ____________

4. ____________

5. ____________

6. ____________

7. ____________

8. ____________

9. ____________

B **Make sentences with the words.**
Schreiben Sie Sätze mit den Wörtern.

Examples:
1. I haven't got a vase in my room.
2. I have got a ... in my room.

1

Dario I live in Birmingham in a big *flat near* the city centre with my parents. My mother is a *housewife* and my father is a train driver. I have got a little sister Laura and a brother Marco. My family came here *ten years ago* from *Italy*. I don't like it so much here: there are *lots of* cars, not many trees and we haven't got a garden. The people in Birmingham are *friendly* but I like Italy more. In the holidays I often go to Italy. My uncle Roberto is a *farmer*, he lives near Rome. My *older* brother Angelo is a *mechanic* in Turin where my *grandparents* live. When I'm older, I want to go back there.

Marie My home is in Dublin in *Ireland*. I love it here: the people are *really* nice and there are many things to do in Dublin. My mother is a *shop assistant* and my father is *out of work*. My little sister is at school. Our house is very old; it's in the city centre, not *far* from the station. All the houses look the same in our street. Our house has got three bedrooms and a small garden where I can sit and talk to the *kids next door*.

A **Fill in the chart below with information from the texts above.**
Vervollständigen Sie die Tabelle (Stichworte).

	Dario	Marie
city ►		
house / flat ►		
garden ►		
family ►		

B **True or false? Mark the boxes with a ✗ to show if the sentence is true or false.**
Richtig oder falsch? Kreuzen Sie an.

	true	false
1. Dario lives with six other people.	☐	☐
2. Dario likes the city where he lives.	☐	☐
3. He doesn't like the people in Birmingham.	☐	☐
4. There are three people in Marie's family.	☐	✗
5. Marie's house is near the station.	☐	☐

flat	Wohnung	**friendly**	nett, freundlich	**really**	wirklich
near	in der Nähe von	**farmer**	Bauer, Farmer	**shop assistant**	Verkäuferin
housewife	Hausfrau	**older**	älter	**out of work**	arbeitslos
ten years ago	vor 10 Jahren	**mechanic**	Mechaniker	**far**	weit (weg/entfernt)
Italy	Italien	**grandparents**	Großeltern	**kids**	Kinder/junge Leute
lots of	viel(e)	**Ireland**	Irland	**next door**	nebenan

C **Find the words in the text about Dario and Marie and write them down.**
Suchen Sie die Wörter im Text und schreiben Sie sie auf.

1. a person who works with animals / in the fields ____________________
2. a person who repairs things ____________________
3. a person who drives a train ____________________
4. your parents' mother and father ____________________
5. a woman who works at home ____________________

D **This is Dario's *family tree*.**
Fill in: – the other *members* of the family
– information about where they live
– information about what they do.
Vervollständigen Sie Darios Familien-Stammbaum.

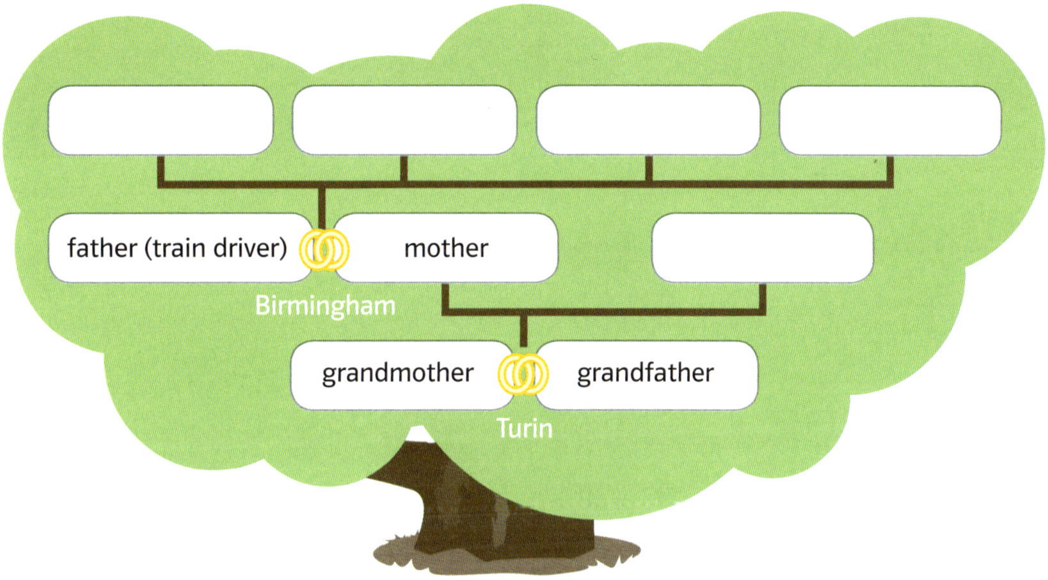

2 **Now draw your own family tree in the same way.**
You may need some of the words in the box.
Zeichnen Sie Ihren eigenen Familien-Stammbaum.
Die Wörter im Kasten sind als Hilfe gedacht.

sister-in-law great grandmother cousin brother-in-law niece nephew great grandfather

3 **Answer the questions about your home. Write down the answers.**
Beantworten Sie die Fragen über Ihr Zuhause.
Schreiben Sie die Antworten auf.

1. Where do you live?
2. Do you live in a house or a flat?
3. What is it like?
4. How many rooms are there?
5. Have you got a garden?
6. Have you got a *balcony*?
7. Who do you live with?
8. What do you like about your home?

field Feld
family tree Familien-Stammbaum
member Mitglied
sister-in-law Schwägerin
great grandmother Urgroßmutter
cousin Cousin, Cousine
brother-in-law Schwager
niece Nichte
nephew Neffe
great grandfather Urgroßvater
balcony Balkon

4 A Name the parts of this house and the things in it. Use the words in the box.
Benennen Sie die Dinge in diesem Haus. Benutzen Sie die Wörter im Kasten.

window *carpet* *curtains* *wardrobe* *cupboard* *cooker*
armchair *fridge* *upstairs* *chest of drawers*
downstairs *coffee table* *lamp*

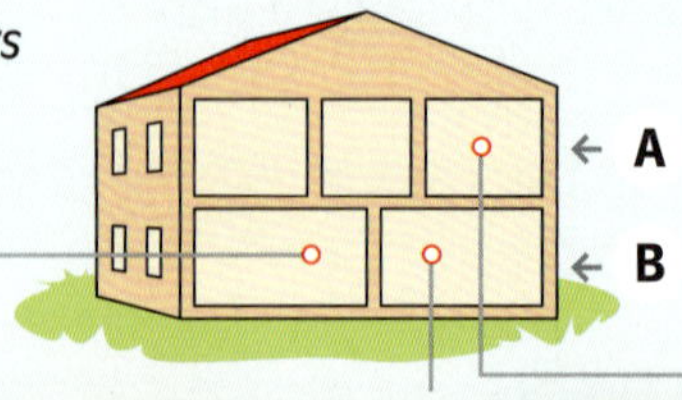

B Complete the following sentences about the house.
Vervollständigen Sie die Sätze.

1. There is a fridge in the kitchen.
2. There ________ a lamp in the living room.
3. There ________ three rooms upstairs.
4. There isn't a ________ downstairs.
5. There ________ a fridge in the bedroom.
6. There ________ any *shelves* in the bedroom.

C Complete the following sentences about the house.
Vervollständigen Sie die Sätze.

1. The house has got two *storeys*: an upstairs and a downstairs.
2. The kitchen and bedroom have got windows.
3. The kitchen hasn't got ________ .
4. The bedroom ________ a *washbasin.*
5. The living room and bedroom ________ a carpet.
6. The kitchen and bedroom ________ a TV.

window	Fenster	**upstairs**	oben (im Haus)	**lamp**	(Steh-)Lampe
carpet	Teppich	**downstairs**	unten (im Haus)	**shelf, shelves**	Regal, Regale
curtain	Vorhang	**wardrobe**	Kleiderschrank	**storey**	Etage
armchair	Sessel	**cupboard**	Schrank	**washbasin**	Waschbecken
fridge	Kühlschrank	**chest of drawers**	Kommode		
cooker	Herd	**coffee table**	Couchtisch		

5 A **Draw a simple plan of your house or flat.**
Zeichnen Sie einen einfachen Grundriss Ihres Hauses / Ihrer Wohnung.

B **Now write about your house or flat. Use information from your plan.**
Schreiben Sie über Ihr Haus / Ihre Wohnung. Benutzen Sie den Grundriss als Hilfe.

Examples:
1. There are ... rooms in my ...
2. We have ... in the bathroom.
3. In the kitchen there ...
4. The bedroom hasn't ...
5. There aren't any ...
6. There ... in the *hall*.
7. We ... in the living room.
8. We ...
9. There ...
10. My room ...

C **Ask a partner questions about his / her house or flat. Start your questions as in the examples.**
Stellen Sie sich gegenseitig Fragen. Beginnen Sie wie in den Beispielen.

Examples:
Is there ...? / Are there ...?   Has it got ...? / Have you got ...?

hall Flur

Present tense Gegenwart

► **to be / there is / there are**

Positive Aussage	Verneinung	Frage
I am (I'm) from Ireland. **You are (You're)** from Italy. **He/she/it is (He's/she's/it's)** friendly. **We are (We're)** in the kitchen. **You are (You're)** on the balcony. **They are (They're)** parents.	**I'm not** from Dublin. **You're not** from New York. **He/she/it isn't** from Rome. **We aren't** out of work. **You aren't** a housewife. **They aren't** train drivers.	**Am I** from Italy? **Are you** upstairs? **Is he/she/it** downstairs? **Are we** in the garden? **Are you** in the kitchen? **Are they** on the balcony?
There is (There's) a shelf on the wall. **There are** shelves in the kitchen.	**There isn't** a kitchen upstairs. **There aren't** any chairs in the bathroom.	**Is there** a phone? **Are there** any curtains?

► **has / have got**

Positive Aussage	Verneinung	Frage
I have (I've) got a house. **You have (You've) got** a flat. **He/she/it has (He's/she's/it's) got** a hall. **We have (We've) got** a balcony. **You have (You've) got** a garden. **They have (They've) got** a video.	**I haven't got** a flat. **You haven't got** a house. **He/she/it hasn't got** a new flat. **We haven't got** a brother. **You haven't got** a sister. **They haven't got** a car.	**Have I got** a TV? **Have you got** a DVD player? **Has he/she/it got** a bedroom? **Have we got** a fridge? **Have you got** a telephone? **Have they got** a CD player?

6 A **Listen to Sally. Which of these things does she talk about? Put a ✗ next to the correct words.**
Worüber spricht Sally? Hören Sie zu und kreuzen Sie die richtigen Wörter an.

☐ brother	☐ bed	☐ records	☐ wall	☐ sister	☐ chair
☐ walkman	☐ parents	☐ green	☐ door	☐ CDs	☐ friends
☐ grey	☐ window	☐ shelves	☐ father		

B **Listen to the text again. Who or what is it?**
Hören Sie den Text noch einmal. Wer oder was ist es?

1. He has got a flat now: ______
2. They say she can do what she wants with her room: ______
3. They are blue or green: ______
4. She can *stretch out* on it: ______
5. She can listen to it all the time: ______
6. She can talk to them in her room: ______

7 A **Look at the rooms below. Describe what you can see in each room.**
Beschreiben Sie die Zimmer.

B **Which one looks most like a room you would like to have? Say why you like it.**
Welches Zimmer würden Sie wählen? Warum?

8 A **Read the following part of a poem called HOME.**
Lesen Sie den folgenden Teil des Gedichts HOME.

Home

Home is where you're always wrong –
too fat or too *thin*.
Home's an *endless argument*
you can never win.

Home is where you're *not the way*
they want you to be

B **Now complete the sentences with your ideas about home. (Don't worry if they don't rhyme!)**
Vervollständigen Sie die Sätze mit Ihren Vorstellungen über ein Zuhause. (Sie müssen sich nicht reimen!)

Examples:
1. Home is where …
2. Home is …
3. Home …
4. …

to stretch out sich ausgestreckt hinlegen	**thin** dünn	**argument** Streit
	endless endlos	**not the way** nicht so (wie)

Free time

A **Find the *small ads* which show these places. Write them down.**
Suchen Sie die Kleinanzeigen, die folgende Orte beschreiben.
Schreiben Sie sie auf.

1. You can do sports in ____________________ .
2. You can get something to eat in ____________________ .
3. You can dance in ____________________ .

B **Work with a partner. Find the words in the small ads which mean the following. Write them down.**
Partnerarbeit. Suchen Sie die Wörter in den Kleinanzeigen, die folgende Bedeutung haben. Schreiben Sie sie auf.

1. a place where you can go to eat restaurant
2. a place where there are many shops ________________
3. the day before the weekend ________________
4. a game with two players, a ball and a *net* ________________
5. a group of people who play music ________________
6. food which *Americans* often eat ________________

small ad Kleinanzeige **net** Netz **American** Amerikaner/in

1

Reporter Jodi Hopkins of 'Teen' *magazine* talks to young people about their free time. Today she is talking to Matt Peterson. He is eighteen and lives at home with his mother.

Matt I don't have a job at the moment. *During* the day I do *a bit* of *gardening* for my mum and the *neighbours*. I hope to find a job as a *gardener*. When I was younger, I went to the *cinema* and to parties a lot, but I don't do that now. I've got other things to do.

Jodi Do you *spend* much time *outdoors?*

Matt Yeah. I *sometimes* work on my bike. I work on it *outside* because we haven't got a garage. And I like to *draw* animals and people. They're not *brilliant drawings* but they're okay. I also play football and now baseball – that's a really cool game! We've got our own team here in the *village* – and my girlfriend plays with us when she's got time.

Jodi Isn't it *difficult* to understand the *rules* in baseball?

Matt No – they're not *hard*. There are eighteen players who try to *hit* the ball or catch it and then run back to the place they started from. I *enjoy* baseball. The *atmosphere* is great – like a party really.

A **Find four things Matt does in his free time.**
Schreiben Sie vier Dinge auf, die Matt in seiner Freizeit macht.

____

B **Answer the questions. Write down your answers.**
Beantworten Sie die Fragen. Schreiben Sie Ihre Antworten auf.

1. Where does Matt live? – Example: **He lives at home.**
2. What does he hope to do? ____________
3. What does he work on? ____________
4. What does he draw? ____________
5. What games does Matt play? ____________
6. When does his girlfriend play baseball? ____________

C **Describe the following things – the words are in the text above.**
Schreiben Sie auf, wie folgende Dinge sind. Die Wörter finden Sie oben im Text.

1. Matt's drawings ____________
2. baseball game ____________
3. baseball rules ____________
4. atmosphere at a baseball game ____________

reporter	Reporterin	**to spend**	verbringen	**difficult**	schwierig
magazine	Zeitschrift	**outdoors**	draußen	**rule**	Regel
during	während	**sometimes**	manchmal	**hard**	schwierig
a bit	ein bisschen	**outside**	draußen	**to hit**	schlagen
gardening	Gartenarbeit	**to draw**	zeichnen	**to enjoy**	Spaß haben an
neighbour	Nachbar(-in)	**brilliant**	brillant, toll, genial	**atmosphere**	Stimmung
gardener	Gärtner	**drawing**	Zeichnung		
cinema	Kino	**village**	Dorf		

D **Find words in the text that mean the same. Write them down.**
Suchen Sie Wörter im Text mit derselben Bedeutung.
Schreiben Sie sie auf.

1. now ______________________
2. outside ______________________
3. brilliant ______________________
4. enjoy ______________________
5. hard ______________________
6. a very small town ______________________

2 **Anna is Matt's girlfriend. The pictures show a day in Anna's life.**
Match the activities in the box to the pictures.
Ordnen Sie die Tätigkeiten im Kasten den richtigen Bildern zu.

go to college | go to bed | eat lunch | see Matt | do homework
have breakfast | have a German lesson | get up

1. ______________________
2. ______________________
3. ______________________
4. ______________________
5. ______________________
6. ______________________
7. ______________________
8. ______________________

3 **Look at the photos and write down what the people do in their free time.**
Schauen Sie die Fotos an und schreiben Sie auf, was die Leute in ihrer Freizeit machen.

1. go by . . .

2. send text messages

3. ______

4. ______

5. ______

6. ______

4 **A** **Read the puzzles. Then write down what the people do in their free time.**
Lesen Sie die Rätsel. Schreiben Sie dann auf, was die Leute in ihrer Freizeit machen.

1. Jane I *usually* look in the newspaper. I check *what's on*. I *choose* one I like. I phone a friend and *fix a time*. I *meet* my friend. I buy my ticket and some popcorn. I go into a *large dark* room and *sit down* to watch.

______

2. Pete I get my T-shirt, shorts and *boots*, but I don't put them on. I put them in a bag. I get the ball. I *leave* the house. I don't get the bus, I walk for ten minutes to the park. I don't *stay alone*, I meet my friends there – we are 22 boys. I put on my boots. I walk on the grass. The *whistle* goes. I start to play. I play for 90 minutes.

______

B **Rewrite the two puzzles.**
Schreiben Sie die beiden Rätsel noch einmal. Beginnen Sie so:

Examples:
1. **Jane looks in the newspaper. She checks what's on. . . .**
2. **Pete gets his T-shirt, shorts and boots, but he doesn't put them on. . . .**

to send a text message eine SMS verschicken	**to fix a time** eine Zeit ausmachen	**to sit down** sich hinsetzen
usually normalerweise	**to meet** (sich) treffen (mit)	**boot** Stiefel
what's on was läuft	**large** groß	**to leave** verlassen
to choose aussuchen	**dark** dunkel	**to stay alone** allein bleiben
		whistle Pfeife; Anpfiff

5 A **The same interests and hobbies are *important* when you choose a *mate* (boyfriend or girlfriend). Look at the interests below, mark how often you do them with a *X*.**
Kreuzen Sie an, wie oft Sie folgende Aktivitäten in Ihrer Freizeit machen.

	cinema	*cooking*	music	sport	parties	TV	discos	*dancing*
often	☐	☐	☐	☐	☐	☐	☐	☐
sometimes	☐	☐	☐	☐	☐	☐	☐	☐
never	☐	☐	☐	☐	☐	☐	☐	☐

B **Write down eight questions to interview your partner. You can use the verbs in the box.**
Schreiben Sie acht Fragen für Ihr Interview mit dem Partner / der Partnerin auf.
Die Verben im Kasten sind als Hilfe gedacht.

Example: **Do you often do the cooking?**
Yes, I do. / No, I don't.

watch go go go
go ~~do~~ do listen to

C **Ask him / her the questions and write down his / her answers.**
Stellen Sie Ihre Fragen. Schreiben Sie die Antworten Ihres Partners / Ihrer Partnerin neben Ihre Fragen wie im Beispiel in **5B**.

D **Report your partner's answers.**
Berichten Sie, was Sie über Ihren Partner / Ihre Partnerin herausgefunden haben.

Example:
1. My partner (Thomas) often goes to the cinema.
2. My partner (Thomas) doesn't often do the cooking.

important wichtig
mate Kumpel, Freund/in
cooking Kochen
dancing Tanzen

Present simple Gegenwart

Positive Aussage	Verneinung	Frage
I play baseball.	**I don't watch** tennis.	**Do I like** football?
You play basketball.	**You don't enjoy** football.	**Do you play** tennis?
He/she/it plays volleyball.	**He/she/it doesn't like** hockey.	**Does he/she/it enjoy** basketball?
We play football.	**We don't enjoy** volleyball.	**Do we go** cycling?
You play tennis.	**You don't play** baseball.	**Do you go** shopping?
They play hockey.	**They don't watch** basketball.	**Do they phone** a friend?

Kurzantworten

Do you go to the cinema? Yes, I do.
Does she play basketball? No, she doesn't.

Anwendung

Das present simple steht bei regelmäßigen oder wiederholten Handlungen und Gewohnheiten (oft mit Häufigkeitsadverbien wie often, sometimes, never usw.).

I never eat tomatoes.
He often goes shopping on Saturday.
She usually cooks lunch.
They sometimes visit friends.

6 A Listen to the people. What do they do and what would they like to do? Then fill in the missing information.
Hören Sie zu. Was machen die Leute in ihrer Freizeit? Und was würden sie gerne in Ihrer Freizeit machen? Vervollständigen Sie die Tabelle.

name ►			
job ►			
free time activities ►			
wishes ►			*children's nurse*

B Look at the hobbies and interests below. Choose the best hobby or free time activity for each person in 6A. Mark them with a *X*.
Wählen Sie das beste Hobby bzw. die beste Freizeit-Beschäftigung für die Personen in **6A**. Kreuzen Sie an.

	Max	Liz	Ann
bungee jumping	☐	☐	☐
an evening class	☐	☐	☐
unpaid work at the hospital	☐	☐	☐
a squash club	☐	☐	☐
a *cybercafe*	X	☐	☐
guitar lessons	☐	☐	☐

C Make sentences about the people and the best activities for them.
Schreiben Sie Sätze über die Leute und die besten Aktivitäten für sie.

Example:
A cybercafe would be the right thing for Max because he wants to meet people and he likes computers.

7 Work with a partner. How many words can you find from the letters of the word ATMOSPHERE? You can use all the letters and you can use them more than once.
Partnerarbeit. Wie viele Wörter können Sie aus dem Wort ATMOSPHERE machen? Sie können alle Buchstaben in beliebiger Reihenfolge – und zwar bei jedem Wort wieder – verwenden.

Examples: **OTHER, SET**

8 words = good!
12 words = very good!!
16 words and more = brilliant!!!

exciting spannend, aufregend
wish Wunsch
children's nurse Kinderkrankenschwester
bungee jumping Bungeejumping
unpaid unbezahlt
cybercafe Internet-Café
guitar Gitarre

Image and style 3

A **Lots of words in *style* and *fashion* are the same in German and in English. Look at the photos below and write down the names of each object.**
Schauen Sie die unten stehenden Fotos an und schreiben Sie die Bezeichnungen darunter.

1. ____________________

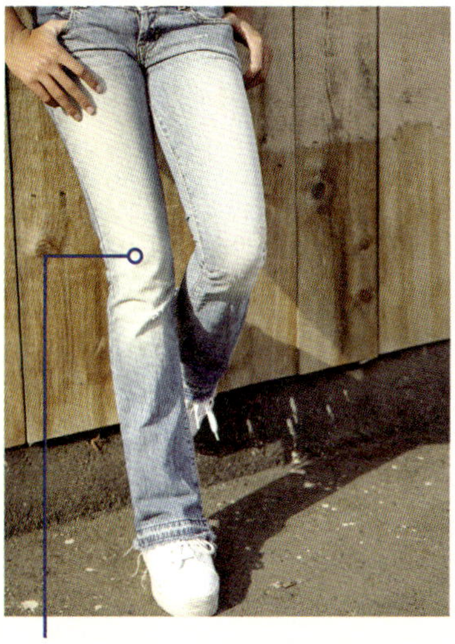

2. ____________________

3. ____________________

4. ____________________

5. ____________________

6. ____________________

B **Say what you are *wearing* today. Then write sentences.**
Sagen Sie was Sie heute tragen. Schreiben Sie dann Sätze.

Example: **I am wearing a jacket.**

style Stil | **fashion** Mode | **to wear** (Kleidung) tragen

1 Talk about style

It's Monday and nine o'clock in Brentridge. A group of *students* at Dean Business *College* are going to their class in Room 312. Their first lesson: English with *Ms* James. But there's no teacher *in sight*. The students are sitting or *standing around*, talking. *A few* are quickly finishing their English homework. Isn't Ms James coming to class today? At five past nine, she *bursts* into the classroom.

Ms James	Morning *everybody*! Sorry I'm late, I had a *problem* with my car. (Ms James looks around the room.)
Ms James	Where's Leyla?
Claire	She's coming in a minute. She *had to* see the school *secretary*.
Ms James	*What about* Mark? Why isn't he here?
Mark	I am here!
Ms James	Oh, sorry Mark. You *look like* Tim.
Mark	I don't.
Ms James	Well, where is Tim?
Mark	He's looking for a *parking space*.
Ms James	And Sue?
Claire	I think she's staying at home today. She didn't feel well yesterday.
Ms James	Okay. Now, today we are talking about *personal style*. Let's begin with what we're wearing. What are you wearing this morning, Danny?
Danny	Jeans, a sweatshirt, shoes and a jacket.
Ms James	Okay. But that doesn't tell us much about your style. What are your jeans like? *Baggy*? *Tight*? Designer? *Second-hand*? And what about your sweatshirt, shoes and jacket? (Ms James looks at the other students in the class.)
Ms James	Hair, make-up and *jewellery* are also important when you talk about style. Can you *describe* your look?

A Answer the following questions. Write down your answer.

Beantworten Sie die Fragen. Schreiben Sie sie auf.

1. Who are the students waiting for?
2. Why is Ms James late?
3. Why is Leyla not in class today?
4. Why is Tim not in class?
5. What is Sue doing today?
6. What is the teacher talking about today?
7. What is Danny wearing this morning?
8. What type of jeans are there?

student Schüler/in
college Berufs(fach)schule
Ms Frau (auch für Unverheiratete)
in sight in Sicht, zu sehen
to stand around herumstehen
a few einige
to burst (herein) platzen
everybody alle, jeder
problem Problem
to have to müssen
secretary Sekretärin
What about ...? Was ist mit ...?
to look like aussehen wie
parking space Parkplatz
personal style persönlicher Stil
baggy sehr weit
tight eng
second-hand gebraucht
jewellery Schmuck
to describe beschreiben

B **Find the words in the text in 1 and write them down.**
Suchen Sie die Wörter im Text in **1** und schreiben Sie sie auf.

1. When you can see *something*, it is ______________________.
2. When you are ill, you don't feel ______________________.
3. The place you park your car is a ______________________.
4. Jeans and a T-shirt are *clothes* you can ______________________.
5. When you say what something or *someone* looks like, you ________________ it/them.

2 **The drawings below are all mixed up. Look at the people.**
Die Zeichnungen unten sind durcheinander geraten.
Schauen Sie die Leute an.

A **Who is really wearing what? Match the right clothes to the people.**
Wer trägt was in Wirklichkeit? Ordnen Sie zu.

	waitress	policeman	secretary	car mechanic
1 head			C	
2 top				
3 *legs*				B

B **Describe in complete sentences what the people in 2A are wearing.**
Beschreiben Sie in ganzen Sätzen, was die Leute in **2A** tragen.

Example: **The waitress is wearing a white *blouse*, . . .**

something etwas	**watch** (Armband-)Uhr	**tights** Strumpfhose
clothes Bekleidung	**leg** Bein	**tie** Schlips, Krawatte
someone jemand	**blouse** Bluse	**trousers** Hose
waitress Bedienung	**skirt** Rock	**overalls** Overall

3 A Zeynep and Daniel are friends. What are they doing? Match the verbs with the activities in the pictures.
Ordnen Sie die Verben den Tätigkeiten zu.

~~put on~~	*look at*	*test*
brush	*try on*	read

1. put on

2. ____

3. ____

4. ____

5. ____

6. ____

B Write sentences about the activities in 3A.
Schreiben Sie Sätze über die Tätigkeiten in **3A**.

Example: **Zeynep is putting on make-up.**

4 Zeynep is going into town with her friend Daniel. They are going to a café. Write down the correct sentences (present continuous).
Schreiben Sie die Sätze richtig auf (Verlaufsform).

1. Zeynep: (Why / you / carry / an *umbrella* today?)
   Example: **Why are you carrying an umbrella today?**
2. Daniel: (I know it / not rain / now.) But you never know.
3. Zeynep: (I / only / *make* / *fun of* you.)
   What about Mark's *driving test*? (When / he / *take* / it?)
4. Daniel: (He / take / it tomorrow.) I *wish* him lots of *luck*.
5. Zeynep: Me, too. (Mark / *still* / help / Joe with his homework?)
6. Daniel: No, he isn't. (Joe / look for / someone to help him.)
7. Zeynep: (Well, I not / help / him / again.) I have no time.
8. Daniel: (When / your parents / go / on holiday?)
9. Zeynep: (They / *not* leave / *until* the weekend.) (you / come / to my party?)
10. Daniel: I don't know. (Who / come?)

to look at	ansehen	**to make fun of**	hänseln, aufziehen	**to wish**	wünschen
perfume	Parfüm	**driving test**	Führerscheinprüfung	**luck**	Glück
to brush	bürsten	**to take a test**	eine Prüfung machen	**still**	(immer) noch
to try on	anprobieren			**not … until**	nicht … vor
to test	testen				
umbrella	Regenschirm				

5 **Pairwork. You are Robert/Janina. Phone your friend.**
Partnerarbeit. Sie übernehmen die Rolle von Robert oder Janina.
Führen Sie ein Telefongespräch auf English.

Janina	Robert
► meldet sich.	
	► grüßt Janina, fragt, was sie gerade macht.
► antwortet, dass sie gerade ihr Zimmer aufräumt.	
	► fragt, was Janina danach macht.
► antwortet, dass sie in die Stadt geht. ► fragt, ob Robert mitkommen möchte.	
	► sagt, dass dies eine gute Idee ist.
► fragt, wann sie sich treffen können.	
	► antwortet „In einer halben Stunde."
► sagt, dass das okay ist.	
	► sagt „Bis dann!"
► sagt „Tschüss".	

6 **Find out which letters are missing and complete the text. Then write the text as a dictation.**
Im folgenden Text fehlen Buchstaben. Welche sind das?
Setzen Sie die Buchstaben ein. Schreiben Sie dann den Text als Diktat.

T__day is a v__ry imp__rtant day. I'm waiting f__r my first j__b int__rvi__w. I'm sitting h__r__ with thr__ __ __th__r p__ __pl__. W__ ar__n't talking, and w__'r__ all v__ry n__rv__us. I'm l__ __king at mys__lf and th__ __th__rs. W__ ar__n't w__aring j__ans, __v__ryb__dy is w__aring tr__us__rs __r a skirt, a shirt and a jack__t. I think my p__rs__nal styl__ is __kay. My hair is l__ng but it l__ __ks g__ __d. I'm n__t w__aring t__ __ much mak__-up. I n__ __d this j__b, and I n__ __d a bit __f g__ __d luck!

to tidy up aufräumen **just now** gerade **See you then!** Bis dann!

Present continuous Verlaufsform der Gegenwart

Positive Aussage	Verneinung	Frage
I am (I'm) going into town.	**I'm not wearing** a skirt.	**Am I wearing** jeans?
You are (You're) tidying up.	**You aren't coming** with me.	**Are you going** to school?
He/she/it is (He's/she's/it's) wearing jeans.	**He/she/it isn't staying** at home.	**Is he/she/it looking** at rings in the window?
We are (We're) talking about style.	**We aren't parking** the car.	**Are we going** to a café?
You are (You're) looking at him.	**You aren't waiting** for Joe.	**Are you meeting** a friend?
They are (They're) going to class.	**They aren't carrying** a bag.	**Are they talking** about make-up?

Anwendung

1. Handlungen, die im Moment stattfinden:	They are wearing old jeans today. The teacher is talking now.
2. Handlungen, die auf einen (gegenwärtigen) Zeitraum begrenzt sind bzw. nicht abgeschlossen sind:	She is living in England this year. We are going to Ireland this week.
3. zukünftige Handlungen (mit Zeitbestimmung):	I am buying an umbrella this afternoon. They are meeting in town at two o' clock.

7 A Listen to the interview. Are the people talking about different jobs?
Hören Sie zu. Sprechen die Leute über verschiedene Berufe?

B Listen again and put a ✗ next to the subjects that Tim and Ann are talking about.
Hören Sie das Interview noch einmal. Kreuzen Sie die Themen an, über die gesprochen wird.

☐ jewellery	☐ food	☐ hair	☐ disco
☐ holidays	☐ school	☐ colours	☐ music

C Listen again and answer the following questions.
Hören Sie die CD noch einmal und beantworten Sie die folgenden Fragen.

1. What does Ann say about *rings* and *earrings*?

____

____

2. What does Tim think about *pony tails*, colours and music?

____

____

____

D What about your style? Write three sentences (or more) about what you like and don't like to wear.
Schreiben Sie drei Sätze (oder mehr) darüber, was Sie gerne / nicht gerne tragen.

8 Look at the small ads about *piercing* and *tattoos*. What do you think?
a) Is piercing important/good/bad for you?
Is it important for your image and style?
b) Are tattoos good to have? Are they important for your image and style?
Was denken Sie über Bodypiercing und Tätowierungen?
Versuchen Sie, die Vor- und Nachteile zu beschreiben.

What kind of …?	Was für …?	**piercing**	Piercing	**painless**	schmerzlos
ring	Ring	**tattoo**	Tätowierung	**blood**	Blut
earring	Ohrring	**professional**	professionell		
pony tail	zusammengebundene Haare (Zopf)	**to cut**	schneiden		
		to staple	tackern		

Friends and problems

4

A lot of youth magazines have a problem page with letters from young people.

Teens Today – Problem page

1 I want to be a car mechanic. I'm not trying to be different but I really love cars! I have got a job in a *garage* on Saturdays. I think I do the job well but all the men laugh at me because I'm a girl. It's so unfair! **Nicola, 17**

2 My mum is from *India* so my *skin* is quite brown. In my new school I have terrible problems with my classmates because I look different. Please help me! **Carol, 17**

3 I don't smoke and so all my mates say I'm still a baby. That's not true! I don't want to smoke! It's my personal style and it's not good for you *anyway*. **Stephen, 16**

4 I really think my girlfriend is great. She is pretty, we have the same interests and I love her very much. But now something is wrong. She wants to spend all her free time with me. I can never go out *without* her, I can't meet my friends alone. I don't know what to do, and I need some help! **Harry, 17**

A **Answer the questions about the letters.**
Beantworten Sie die Fragen über die Briefe.

1. What problem does Harry have?
2. Why do the men in the garage laugh at Nicola?
3. Why doesn't Stephen smoke?
4. What problem does Carol have with her classmates?

B **Match the answers to the letters.**
Ordnen Sie die richtigen Antworten den Briefen zu.

☐ **a)** Tell your class teacher about your problem. Then you can all discuss the situation in class. *Racism* is terrible and we must stop it.

☐ **b)** You have a strong character! What your mates think is not important. *Non-smokers* are cool because they are different!

☐ **c)** It is quite normal that you want to have time *for yourself*. Talk to your girlfriend, explain how you feel – and tell her how much you love her!

☐ **d)** Do the job well! Don't listen to what they say. Talk to your boss and ask him for help.

garage Autowerkstatt
India Indien
skin Haut
anyway außerdem, überhaupt
without ohne
racism Rassismus
non-smoker Nichtraucher/in
for yourself für dich (selbst)

1 Problems at work

Nick Millson is seventeen. After he finished school, he began to *train* as a *painter* with a small *company* in his town. He thought he was very lucky because many of his friends didn't have a job. But then the *trouble* started. He couldn't do *anything* right for his *boss*. He made some mistakes, *of course* – but he was new. His boss said things like, "if you don't do better, you'll have to look for a different job." Nick *became* very *nervous* and made *even more* mistakes. He didn't know what to think. He came to work *on time*. He wasn't very *fast* – but an eight-hour day was long and he *soon* got *tired*. Before the first six months were *over*, Nick *lost* his job and started at college. That was *hard* for him. But he knew that he could always talk to his best friend, Alex. *Both* of them played basketball on the same team, but they didn't go to the same school. Alex wanted to go to *university*. Nick didn't really enjoy school. He wanted to do something *practical* and he wanted to *earn* money. After basketball they often talked about their problems.

A Choose the correct answer and underline it.

Wählen Sie die richtige Antwort aus und unterstreichen Sie sie.

1. Nick Millson is
a) twenty years old.
b) under twenty.
c) over twenty.

2. He began to train as
a) a teacher.
b) a policeman.
c) a painter.

3. Nick had trouble at work because
a) the boss didn't like his work.
b) he was too fast.
c) he was always *late*.

4. Nick lost his job
a) in the first month.
b) in the first six months.
c) after one year.

5. Alex was
a) Nick's brother
b) Nick's *neighbour*.
c) Nick's friend.

6. Nick and Alex both played
a) basketball.
b) handball.
c) football.

B Complete the sentences with the correct verbs from the text in 1.

Vervollständigen Sie die Sätze mit den richtigen Verben aus dem Text in **1**.

1. After he finished school last year, Nick began to train as a painter.

2. He and Alex often talked about their problems after basketball.

3. Nick ____________ that he wanted to work.

4. He thought he ____________ very lucky.

5. He ____________ at college.

6. He ____________ to work on time.

7. He ____________ his job.

C Put the sentences in 1B in the order as in the text.

Ordnen Sie die Sätze in **1B** in der Reihenfolge wie im Text.

1. ___ **2.** 4 **3.** ___ **4.** ___ **5.** ___ **6.** ___ **7.** ___

to train	ausgebildet werden	**nervous**	nervös	**hard**	hart
painter	Maler	**even more**	noch mehr	**both**	beide
company	Firma	**on time**	pünktlich	**university**	Universität
trouble	Ärger, Probleme	**fast**	schnell	**practical**	praktisch
not ... anything	nichts	**soon**	bald	**to earn**	verdienen
boss	Chef	**tired**	müde	**to be late**	zu spät kommen
of course	natürlich	**over**	vorbei	**neighbour**	Nachbar
to become	werden	**to lose**	verlieren		

2 Alex and Nick are talking about Nick's problems.

Alex Sorry you lost your job. What *happened*?
Nick I don't know what *went wrong*. But I had a lot of problems with my boss.
Alex Didn't he like you? Or did you come late?
Nick No, I was never late. My mother always *woke me up*. My boss didn't think I was *interested*. I **was** interested in the job but I don't *smile* all the time.
Alex I think he didn't understand you.
Nick Yes. Now I'm at college. It's easier than my job, but I don't have so much money now.
Alex Do you want to leave college?
Nick Of course! I want a job. But what can I do?
Alex There's a job at the supermarket.
Nick Oh, really? How much do they pay?
Alex I don't know. The work's hard, and you can't get your college qualification. What about a job at the weekends to earn some money?
Nick Yes, but then I can't go out on Friday night, and Friday night is disco night!
Alex Well, as I see it, you have three *possibilities*: you can *concentrate* on college, you can stay at college and work at the weekends or you can take a job and leave college.
Nick Yes, I must think about it.

A **Answer the questions about the text.**
Beantworten Sie die Fragen über den Text.

1. Why did Nick lose his job?
2. Was Nick late for work?
3. Who woke him up?
4. Which is easier for Nick – work or college?
5. Does Nick want to leave college?
6. Where could he work?
7. What is good about college?

B **Look at the text. Write down the advantages ⊕ and the disadvantages ⊖ of the three possibilities that Nick has.**
Schauen Sie den Text an. Schreiben Sie die Vor- und Nachteile der drei Möglichkeiten auf, die Nick hat (in Stichworten).

1. college only
2. work at the supermarket
3. college and weekend job

advantage ⊕: . . .
disadvantage ⊖: . . .

C **What would you do in the same situation? Write some sentences and say why.**
Was würden Sie tun? Warum? Schreiben Sie einige Sätze.

to happen passieren
to go wrong schief gehen
to wake someone up jemanden wecken
interested interessiert
to smile lächeln
possibility Möglichkeit
to concentrate sich konzentrieren
advantage Vorteil
disadvantage Nachteil

3 Colin and Angie met, *fell in love, got married* and started a family some years ago.

A **Look at the pictures. Match the verbs and the words from the boxes to the drawings.**
Ordnen Sie die Verben und Wörter aus den beiden Kästen den Zeichnungen zu.

~~meet~~ go cook drive get married have

a baby boy to the cinema ~~at a party~~ spaghetti to London after two years

1. meet at a party
2. ______
3. ______
4. ______
5. ______
6. ______

B **Write Colin and Angie's story.**
Schreiben Sie Colins und Angies Geschichte.

Example: **Colin and Angie met at a party.**

C **Don and Sandra also met, fell in love, got married and had a baby. But everything is a bit different. Write sentences as in 3B.**
Schreiben Sie Sätze wie in 3B.

1. meet / at a disco
   Example: **Don and Sandra didn't meet at a party, they met at a disco.**
2. go / *swimming*
3. cook / hamburgers
4. drive / to Amsterdam
5. get married / after one year
6. have / a baby girl

to fall in love	sich verlieben	**to get married**	heiraten	**swimming**	Schwimmen

4 Maxine calls her friend Julia on the telephone. She says she tried to phone Julia the day before but she wasn't there. Maxine wants to know where Julia was and what she did yesterday.

A **Write Maxine's questions and Julia's short answers*.**
Schreiben Sie Maxines Fragen und Julias Kurzantworten* auf.
*Example: **Yes, I did. / No, I didn't.**

1. go shopping ⊕ Example: **Did you go shopping? Yes, I did.**
2. buy a CD ⊖
3. buy a magazine ⊕
4. *post* a letter ⊖
5. have a coffee ⊕
6. see any of our friends ⊕

B **Julia and Maxine talk about Maxine's evening. Complete the questions.**
Vervollständigen Sie die Fragen.

Maxine James came to see me yesterday.

Julia Why ______________________ to see you?
Maxine I wanted to talk to him about the English *project*.

Julia Why ______________________ to talk to him about the English project?
Maxine I thought that James could help me.

Julia Why ______________________ that James could help you?
You know that he's not so good at English.
Maxine Yes, but I think James is the nicest boy in the class.
Julia He's too nice for you.
Maxine *Thanks a lot!* Who needs friends like you?

to post abschicken **project** Projekt **Thanks a lot!** Vielen Dank!

Past simple Einfache Vergangenheit

Positive Aussage

Angie	cook**ed**	spaghetti	yesterday.
Bill	play**ed**	football	last Monday.

► Grundform (Infinitiv) + **-ed**

Verneinung

Angie	**did not (didn't) drink**	tea.
We	**did not (didn't) write**	a letter.

Frage

Did	you	**see**	your brother?
Did	they	**talk**	about football?

Besonderheiten
y wird zu **ie** tr**y** – tr**ied**

Unregelmäßige Verben
go – **went** meet – **met**

Bei unregelmäßigen Verben wird die 2. Form für das past simple verwendet.

Anwendung
Sally **spoke** to Tim yesterday.
First she **rang** her friend, Joe.
David and Jane **met** in 2005.

Das past simple steht bei Handlungen zu einem bestimmten Zeitpunkt oder in einem abgeschlossenen Zeitraum in der Vergangenheit (oft mit einer Zeitbestimmung wie z. B. yesterday, last year, in 2005, ... ago).

5 Problem situations

a) Sue didn't tell anyone that she was *unhappy* at college. She didn't go to her lessons.
b) George's father often hit him so he *ran away* and lived on the streets.
c) Ben took some CDs from a shop but didn't pay for them.
d) Mark drank too much and couldn't get up for work.
e) Pamela took some ecstasy at a disco and felt *terrible*.

Keep out of trouble!
Tips for young people

1 Don't *steal*.
2 Say 'no' to *drugs*.
3 Don't get *addicted*.
4 Ask for help when you are *worried*.
5 Call an *emergency number* if you are *abused* or *badly treated* at home.

A Read and then match the tips and the problem situations.
Lesen Sie die Tipps und ordnen Sie sie den Situationen zu.

1. ___ 2. ___ 3. ___ 4. a) 5. ___

B What do you think happened next to Sue, George, Ben, Mark and Pamela?
Wie ging es weiter mit Sue, George, Ben, Mark und Pamela? Was meinen Sie?

1. Sue didn't get her qualifications.
2. ______
3. ______
4. ______
5. ______

C Listen to two young people who are talking about their lives. Fill in the table.
Hören Sie die CD. Vervollständigen Sie die Tabelle.

	first speaker	second speaker
name ►		
age ►		
problem ►		
consequences ►		

unhappy unglücklich
to run away weglaufen
terrible schrecklich
to steal stehlen
drug Droge
addicted abhängig
to be worried sich Sorgen machen
emergency number Notruf
abused missbraucht
badly treated misshandelt
consequence Konsequenz, Folge
to fit passen
to kick someone off jemanden rausschmeißen
pill Tablette, Pille
to get caught erwischt werden

Music and media

5

A **How many different *kinds* of music do you know? Put the letters in the box in the right order. The correct words will be different kinds of music. Write them down around the CD.**
Wie viele verschiedene Musikarten kennen Sie? Ordnen Sie die Buchstaben der Wörter im Kasten. Schreiben Sie dann die Musikarten auf.

1. lubes	**6.** losu
2. pihpoh	**7.** pra
3. etohnc	**8.** pnuk
4. cork	**9.** yveha tlmae
5. gergae	**10.** opp smicu

1. blues

2. hiphop

3. ____________________

4. ____________________

5. ____________________

6. ____________________

7. ____________________

8. ____________________

9. ____________________

10. ____________________

B **What do you think? What kind of music do the people in the photos like? Write down the kind of music they *probably* like.**
Was denken Sie? Welche Art von Musik gefällt den Leuten auf den Fotos? Schreiben Sie die Art von Musik auf der Schreibzeile.

1. ____________________

2. ____________________

3. ____________________

C **What kind of music do you like?**
Welche Art von Musik gefällt Ihnen?

media Medien **kind** Art **probably** wahrscheinlich

1 A NEW STAR

Pop *stars* come and go. But Katie Melua from *Britain* is going to be here for a long time.

Katie Melua was *born* in *Georgia* in Eastern Europe in 1984. Her family went to *Belfast* in Northern Ireland when Katie was 8 years old. They left Georgia because Katie's father, a doctor, got a new job in a Belfast hospital in 1992. Katie went to school in Northern Ireland until she was 13. Then her family *moved* again. This time they went to London, where Katie finished school. Then she went to the *Brit College for Performing Arts*. At college some pop music *producers* *discovered* her talent. Katie started to make some *successful* CDs. She had some number one *hits* and *appeared* on many shows on TV. She *brought out* her first *album* "Call off the Search" in Britain in 2003.

Katie also thinks that she can help a lot of people in the world *through* her work as a pop star. So she sings in concerts for different *charities*. For example, in 2004 she sang at a concert to help poor children in Sri Lanka. What is Katie going to do next? Is she going to be more successful? Is her music going to become different? *Whatever* happens in the *future*, we hope that Katie is going to make music for a long time.

Katie Melua

A Put the pictures in the order of the text and number them.

Ordnen Sie die Bilder in der Reihenfolge des Textes. Schreiben Sie die Nummer in die Kästchen.

☐

☐

☐

☐

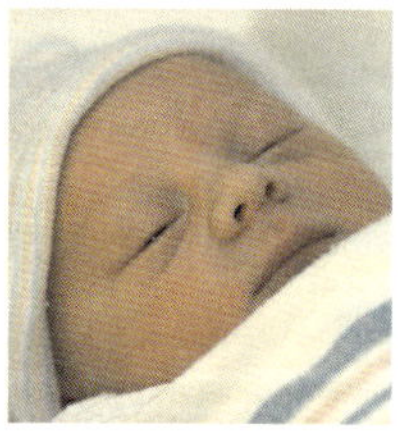

1

B Write the sentences in the text which match the pictures in 1A.

Schreiben Sie die Sätze aus dem Text auf, die zu den Abbildungen in 1A gehören.

Example: **1. Katie Melua was born in Georgia in 1984.**

star Star
Britain Großbritannien
born geboren
Georgia Georgien
Belfast Stadt in Nordirland
to move umziehen
Brit College for Performing Arts Musik- und Schauspielschule in England
producer Produzent
to discover entdecken
successful erfolgreich
hit Hit
to appear Gast sein
to bring out herausbringen
album Album
through durch
charity wohltätiger Zweck
whatever was auch immer
future Zukunft

C **Answer the following questions.**
Beantworten Sie folgende Fragen.

1. How old was Katie when she left Eastern Europe?
2. Why did her family move to Northern Ireland?
3. When did Katie's family go to London?
4. What did Katie do after school?
5. Who discovered Katie?
6. How does Katie help other people?

D **Write about another young singer, Jamie Cullum. Use the words below.**
Schreiben Sie einen kurzen Text über den Sänger Jamie Cullum.
Benutzen Sie die angegebenen Wörter.

1. born in Malmesbury, England in 1979
2. mother from *Burma*, father from *Israel*
3. school in Malmesbury until he was 18
4. study English and film at university
5. sing in *pubs* to make money
6. meet an important music producer
7. have a successful CD last year
8. become a bigger star in the future

2 **Look at the *row* of four shops and a cinema in Compton High Street. Find out who *owns* them. Write down your solution.**
Lesen Sie alle Informationen über die Besitzer der Läden und des Kinos. Wer hat welchen Laden und wem gehört das Kino? Schreiben Sie Ihre Lösung auf.

The owners of the cinema and shops are:
Susy Pace (who doesn't have the *DVD shop*)
Joe Bean (who doesn't have the *newsagent's*)
Mike Marvel (who doesn't have the computer shop)
Tom Turner (who doesn't have the cinema)
Dave Diggins (who doesn't have the CD shop)

Dave Diggins owns one of the shops at the end of the row. Mike Marvel's shop is *next to* the cinema. Mike Marvel is a good friend of the newsagent and hopes that she will sell him her shop one day.

Susy Pace owns ... ______
Joe Bean ______
Mike Marvel ______
Tom Turner ______
Dave Diggins ______

Burma	Birma	**row**	Reihe	**newsagent's**	Zeitungskiosk
Israel	Israel	**owner**	Besitzer/in	**to own**	besitzen
pub	Kneipe	**DVD shop**	DVD Verleih	**next to**	neben

3 **Look at the pictures and use the verbs in the box. Write down what the people are going to do.**
Schreiben Sie, was die Leute jetzt gleich machen werden. Benutzen Sie die Verben im Kasten.

sing *switch on*
drink listen make

1. She's going to make a phone call.
2. ______
3. ______
4. ______
5. ______

4 **Read the group's *press release*. Ask your partner questions about the group. He / she gives the answers.**
Lesen Sie die Pressemitteilung der Gruppe.

Press Release

name of group:	Blueday
name of next album:	Blueday Hits
date of *release*:	15/06
record label:	MRL
dates of next *tour*:	April-September
countries on tour:	Britain, Germany, France, Spain

1. What (call / next album) are they going to call their next record?
   They're going to call it "Blueday Hits".

to switch on	einschalten	**release**	Neuerscheinung	**tour**	Tournee
press release	Pressemitteilung	**record label**	Plattenfirma		

2. When (*release* it) ______________________________ ?

____

3. What label (record / it on) ______________________________ ?

____

4. When (start / their tour) ______________________________ ?

____

5. When (end / their tour) ______________________________ ?

____

6. What (countries / tour in) ______________________________ ?

____

5 **Read the sentences. Write down what the people are <u>not</u> going to do the next time.**
Lesen Sie die Sätze. Schreiben Sie auf, was die Leute beim nächsten Mal nicht tun werden.

1. Mark and Tim watched a *violent* film. They felt ill.
   They're not going to . . . ______________________________ .
2. Sally listened to a CD by Blueday. She didn't like it.
   ______________________________ .
3. Ann and Paul went to see a western. It was boring.
   ______________________________ .
4. Ella bought a very cheap DVD in the shop. The pictures were very bad.
   ______________________________ .

to release herausbringen **violent** gewalttätig

Going to-future going-to-Zukunft

Positive Aussage	Verneinung	Frage
I'm going to post the letter. **You're going to** listen to pop music. **He / she / it's going to** watch a concert. **We're going to** cook dinner. **You're going to** enjoy the music. **They're going** to buy a DVD.	**I'm not going to** post the card. **You're not going to** listen to reggae. **He / she / it isn't going to** watch a film. **We aren't going to** sing. **You aren't going to** enjoy the film. **They aren't going to** buy a book.	**Am I going to** make a coffee? **Are you going to** listen to rock music? **Is he / she / it going to** watch a DVD? **Are we going to** eat dinner? **Are you going to** do homework after school? **Are they going to** buy CDs?

Anwendung
Bei Absicht und Vorhaben:

Graham is going to watch football on TV this evening.
Tracey is going to sing in a concert on Saturday.

6 A Listen to the dialogue on CD. Fill in the missing information in the TV guide.
Hören Sie den Dialog auf der CD. Vervollständigen Sie das TV-Programm.

SATURDAY EVENING TV

BBC1

6.00	News and weather
6.__	Mr Bean
7.00	Top of the Pops
7.30	Wild animals in Africa
9.00	Mario and the ______

ITV

6.30	National and local news
7.30	Coronation Street
8.00	The ______
8.30	Britain's richest ______
9.30	Live in concert: Katie Melua

BBC2

6.15	The Simpsons
7.00	World darts
7.__	**Film** A night to remember Another Monster film!
9.45	Have I got ______ for you!
10.15	Newsnight
11.00	**Film** Lost in time

Channel Four

6.00	News quiz
6.30	Planet football
7.30	News and weather
8.30	**Film** What happened last ______ ?
10.35	**Film** Blueday – The movie

B Listen to the CD again and complete the sentences.
Hören Sie den Dialog noch einmal und vervollständigen Sie die Sätze.

1. Liz is tired because ______________________.
2. Jeff was late because ______________________.
3. Jeff bought a newspaper so ______________________.
4. They can't watch 'Mr Bean' because ______________________.
5. Jeff wants to do the cooking because ______________________.

7 What are you (not) going to watch on TV at the weekend? Why? Use the words in the box. Check them in a dictionary.
Was sehen Sie (nicht) am Wochenende im Fernsehen? Warum?
Benutzen Sie die Wörter im Kasten, die Wortliste oder ein Wörterbuch.

Example: **I'm going to watch … because it's funny.**
I'm not going to watch … because it's boring.

action film comedy crime story current affairs programme detective series documentary music show romantic film science-fiction *soap* sports series thriller quiz show

funny boring sentimental frightening interesting exciting

soap Seifenoper

London 6

A **Look at the photos on the right. Match them with the suitable word or words from the box.**
Schauen Sie sich die Bilder auf der rechten Seite an und ordnen Sie diese den Begriffen im Kasten zu.

Stop and Go *Rush Hour* Tourist Information *Guide*
Musical Hi Tickets *Lift* Service Bus
Hotel Shopping Park Clubs Action cool

a) ____________

b) ____________

c) ____________

d) ____________

B **Complete the "German" email. Use words from the box.**
Vervollständigen Sie das deutsche E-Mail. Verwenden Sie dazu Wörter aus dem Kasten.

Von: Simone Bauer s.bauer@cool.eu
An: bine@cool.eu; gabi.meyer@cool.eu; timo@cool.eu
Betreff: Wenn ihr mal richtig was erleben wollt …

(1) ________ Leute!!!

Wenn ihr mal richtig was erleben wollt, dann fahrt nach London. Hier gibt's jede Menge (2) ________ . Schon wenn man vom Flughafen mit dem (3) ________ in die Stadt kommt, sieht alles total (4) ________ aus. Allerdings – bei dem vielen Verkehr besonders in der (5) ________ dauert's natürlich lange – ständig (6) ________ . Zuerst sind wir zur (7) ________ und haben uns da einen (8) ________ gekauft. Sie haben uns auch erzählt, wo man günstig (9) ________ für ein (10) ________ bekommt. Wir hatten ja schon ein billiges (11) ________ gebucht. Wir wohnen im 5. Stock, aber sie haben glücklicherweise einen (12) ________ . Und das Personal im Hotel ist sehr nett und der (13) ________ ist nicht übel. Gerade waren wir (14) ________ in Oxford Street, jetzt erholen wir uns hier im (15) ________ , man darf hier sogar den Rasen betreten! Heute Abend werden wir einen der vielen (16) ________ besuchen. Sie sollen sehr voll sein.

Bis bald, Simone

stop and go traffic stockender Verkehr
rush hour Hauptverkehrszeit
guide Reiseführer
lift Aufzug

1

LONDON

Insider tips for young people

See interesting things, dance *all night*, go to clubs … all you need is some *pocket money*.

Tip 1
YHA

Cheap *youth hostel* near Oxford Street. Two-bed and four-bed rooms. Stay for a maximum of six nights in summer, two weeks in winter. £15 *per* night plus £3 for breakfast.

14–16 Noel Street,
Oxford Circus

Tip 2
Food for *Thought*

Popular *vegetarian* restaurant. *Delicious* meals at *low* prices.

31 Neal Street,
Covent Garden

Tip 3
Bands live on stage

In London you can hear more good bands in a week than on the *continent* in a month! Brixton Academy,

211 Stockwell Road,
Brixton

Tip 4
Sightseeing by bus

You go *sightseeing* on one of the red *double-decker* buses. Start at Oxford Street, go on to St. Paul's, then to Victoria and finish at Piccadilly Circus. Buy a *one-day travelcard*.

Tip 5
Flea markets

If you like shopping at *flea markets*, don't go to Portobello or Camden market. They are *crowded* with tourists. Try Brick Lane market on Sunday morning where you can meet Londoners looking for clothes and other things.

Brick Lane market,
Liverpool Street

Tip 6
Rock Circus

At Rock Circus you can see *wax models* of the Beatles or Madonna. And you can watch a 30-minute show, in which they really move and sing! £8.25.

London Pavilion,
Piccadilly Circus

Tip 7
Street fashion

Street style is made in London! Visit Hype DF where you can find clothes made by tomorrow's star designers.

48–58 High Street
Kensington,
High Street Kensington

= Underground station

all night die ganze Nacht
pocket money Taschengeld
YHA Jugendherbergsvereinigung
youth hostel Jugendherberge
per pro
thought Gedanke
vegetarian vegetarisch
delicious lecker
low niedrig
continent Kontinent
to go sightseeing Sehenswürdigkeiten anschauen
double-decker Doppeldecker
one-day travelcard Tagesfahrkarte
flea market Flohmarkt
crowded voll (mit Menschen)
wax model Wachsfigur

A **Look at the tips for young people in 1 and the photos. Match the pictures with the suitable tips.**
Schauen Sie die Tipps für junge Leute in **1** und die Fotos an. Ordnen Sie die Bilder den passenden Tipps zu.

picture A: ____________

picture B: ____________

picture C: ____________

picture D: ____________

B **Answer the following questions on the text in 1.**
Beantworten Sie die Fragen zum Text in **1**.

Where can you

1. eat? ____________

2. sleep? ____________

3. see interesting things? ____________

4. hear something interesting? ____________

5. buy things? ____________

C **Which offers are free?**
Welche Angebote kosten nichts?

____

____

2 **You are in London for one week. You have £100 left after you have paid for the youth hostel and food. What would you like to do with this money?**
Was möchten Sie mit diesem Geld machen?

3 **PROJECT**
Write insider tips in English for your home town. Think of places where young people can stay for the night, eat and drink, see interesting things or go shopping.
Schreiben Sie Insider-Tipps für Ihre Heimatstadt.
Schlagen Sie vor, wo junge Leute übernachten können, essen und trinken, interessante Dinge sehen oder einkaufen können.

4 **Sally and Harry are in London. What do you think they will do in the following situations?**
Was werden Sally und Harry wohl in folgenden Situationen machen?

1. They want to take a bus to Hyde Park.

Sally: "I haven't got *enough* money for the bus."

Harry: "I'll (will) *lend* you some."

2. They don't know the way to Buckingham Palace.

Harry: "There's a policeman!"

Sally: ______________________

____

3. They are in their hotel room.

Sally: "The phone's ringing!"

Harry: ______________________

____

4. They want to eat in a restaurant.

Waiter: "I'm sorry. We haven't got a table free."

Harry: ______________________

____

5. They want to go to Tower Bridge, so they talk to their hotel *receptionist*.

Harry: "We'd like to walk to Tower Bridge. How far is it?"

Receptionist: "Oh, about three *miles*."

Sally: ______________________

____

5 **What do you think the people will do? Answer the questions.**
Was werden die Leute wohl machen? Beantworten Sie die Fragen.

1. A tourist needs some English money. Where will he go?

I think he'll / he will go to a bank.

2. A woman needs to find her way in London. What will she probably buy?

I think she'll buy ...

enough	genug	**receptionist**	Dame / Herr am Empfang
to lend	leihen	**mile**	Meile (ca. 1,6 km)
to wait	warten		

3. Some boys from Kensington are *packing* old clothes, old books and CDs into boxes. Where do you think they will go?

4. Three girls from Germany need to go to Piccadilly Circus. Will they take the bus or the underground?

5. Two students need a cheap room for the night. Where do you think they will stay?

6 **Two of your friends want to go to London. Give them some tips.**
Zwei Ihrer Freunde wollen nach London reisen. Geben Sie ihnen ein paar Tipps.

1. go to "Food for Thought" / get a delicious meal
   Example: **If you go to "Food for Thought", you will get a delicious meal.**
2. find cheap clothes / go to a flea market
   Example: **You will find cheap clothes if …**
3. go to Rock Circus / see wax models of famous pop stars
4. save money / go sightseeing on a double-decker bus
5. find clothes made by tomorrow's star designers / go to Hype DF
6. see bands on stage / go to Brixton Academy

to pack (zusammen)packen

Will-Future Zukunft

Positive Aussage	Verneinung
I'll (will) go to England.	**I won't (will not) go** to Ireland.
You'll (will) take a bus.	**You won't (will not) buy** things.
He'll / she'll / it'll (will) ask a policeman.	**He / she / it won't (will not) walk.**
We'll (will) see the Tower.	**We won't (will not) take** photos.
You'll (will) buy things.	**You won't (will not) see** the Palace.
They'll (will) go shopping.	**They won't (will not) go** to a club.

Anwendung

Wenn man spontan entscheidet, etwas zu tun:	I'll lend you some money.
Wenn man Vermutungen über die Zukunft anstellt:	I think he'll go to the bank.

Conditional sentences Bedingungssätze

if-Satz (present simple)	**Hauptsatz** (will-future)
If you go by bus,	you'll (will) save money.

Der if-Satz kann am Anfang stehen und wird durch Komma abgetrennt.

Hauptsatz (will-future)	**if-Satz** (present simple)
You'll (will) save money	if you go by bus.

Der if-Satz kann aber auch am Satzende stehen. In diesem Falle wird kein Komma gesetzt.

7 A Listen to four travel announcements. Which announcement is about a plane?
Hören Sie vier Durchsagen für Reisende. Welche Durchsage betrifft ein Flugzeug?

B Listen to the four travel announcements again. Complete the chart.
Hören Sie die vier Durchsagen für Reisende noch einmal. Vervollständigen Sie die Tabelle (in Stichworten).

	1	2	3	4
What's the name of the place? ►	Dover			
Which *means of transport* is used? ►				
Why is it late? ►				
Where do the *passengers* want to go? ►	Calais			

8 You have just been to Rock Circus. You are at Piccadilly Circus underground station. Look at the London underground map and say / write how you will get to the following.
Schauen Sie auf die Londoner U-Bahn-Karte. Wie kommen Sie zu folgenden Orten?

1. Food for Thought **2.** the youth hostel **3.** Brick Lane market

- Which line will you take?
- Where will you *change*?
- Where will you leave the underground?

Look again at the insider tips on page 36!

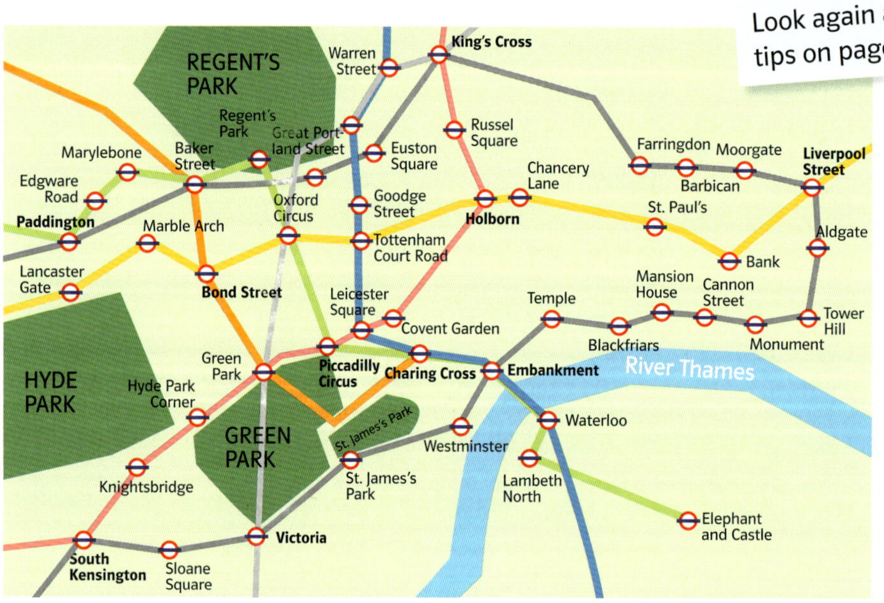

Circle Line
Piccadilly Line
Victoria Line
Jubilee Line
Bakerloo Line
Northern Line
Central Line

means of transport Verkehrsmittel
passenger Passagiere
ferry Fähre
engine Maschine, Motor
flight Flug
delay Verspätung
snow Schnee
breakdown Panne
direction Richtung
to change umsteigen

Different cultures, different people? 7

A **Name the colours. Use the letters in the box.**
Wie heißen die Farben? Benutzen Sie die Buchstaben im Kasten.

kbcal ~~epuplr~~ knip dre
uleb weith erneg

1. purple
2. ______
3. ______
4. ______
5. ______
6. ______
7. ______

B **Work with a partner. Answer the following questions.**
Partnerarbeit. Beantworten Sie folgende Fragen.

What colour are you … when you're born?
… when you *grow up*?
… when you're *sick*?
… when you go in the sun?

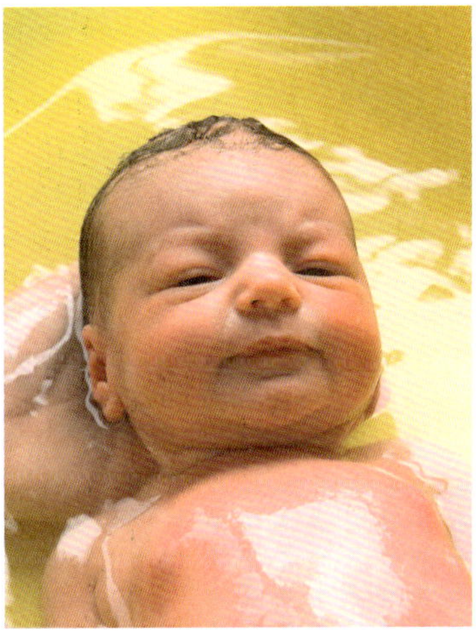

C **Now listen to a rap. What colour is the rapper?**
Hören Sie einen Rap. Welche Hautfarbe hat der Rapper?

D **How does the writer of the text feel? Underline one of the words in the box. Say why you have chosen this word.**
Wie fühlt sich der Verfasser des Textes? Unterstreichen Sie eins der Wörter im Kasten. Warum haben Sie dieses Wort ausgesucht?

frustrated sad happy *afraid* *worried* angry

to grow up erwachsen werden
sick krank
to guess raten, schätzen
to turn red rot werden
to have (got) the nerve die Frechheit haben
frustrated frustriert
afraid ängstlich
worried besorgt

1 A Read the dialogue below and write the names under the photos.

Lesen Sie den Dialog schnell durch. Schreiben Sie die Namen unter die Fotos.

______	______	**Melanie**	______
Parents are *Turkish*, but he is *German* now.	Parents are both German but they were born in *Russia*.	Father is German, mother is *Indian*. They live in *Germany*.	Parents are both American. He has just arrived in Germany.

Outside their company building at *lunchtime*.

Melanie: What about going to the disco *tonight*?
Shane: Why not? But how are we going *to get there*?
Melanie: *By bus*, of course.
Shane: Oh no. … Who could drive us there?
Natalie: Well, my mother hasn't got a *driving licence*. We never had money for a car in Russia. And anyway, it's Wednesday.
Melanie: *So what?*
Natalie: My parents say that I can go out at the weekend, but not during the week.
Fatih: *At least* you can go out at the weekend. My parents have said that I can't go to the disco *at all*.
Shane: I've never heard of anything like that before. Why don't they let you go there?
Fatih: Some Turkish parents think the disco isn't a good place.
Shane: Oh!
Fatih: It isn't so bad. My parents do everything for me. They're really nice.
Shane: My parents too. But they're in America. I *miss* them. I live here now – and go out a lot in the evenings! So … what about Friday evening? Ten o'clock?
Fatih: You can come to my flat first. My mother will make us a *fantastic* Turkish *meal*.
Melanie: Brilliant.
Natalie: Okay. But I'm going to bring some blinis.
Shane: What are they?
Natalie: They're *Russian pancakes*.
Shane: Hey, great. Then I'll bring some *peanut butter cookies*.
Melanie: And I'll ask my parents if they can drive us to the disco.

B Answer the questions in sentences.

Beantworten Sie die Fragen in ganzen Sätzen.

1. Where are the four people?
2. Who hasn't got a driving licence?
3. What does Fatih say about his parents?
4. Where can they go before the disco?
5. Who will bring some peanut butter cookies?

Turkish	türkisch	**to get there**	hinkommen	**fantastic**	fantastisch
German	deutsch	**by bus**	mit dem Bus	**meal**	Essen
Russia	Russland	**driving licence**	Führerschein	**Russian pancake**	russischer Pfannkuchen
Indian	indisch	**So what?**	Ja und?	**peanut butter cookie**	Erdnussbutterkeks
Germany	Deutschland	**at least**	wenigstens		
lunchtime	mittags	**not … at all**	überhaupt nicht		
tonight	heute Abend	**to miss**	vermissen		

C **Read the text again and underline the correct parts.**
Lesen Sie den Text und unterstreichen Sie die richtigen Teile.

1. Natalie, Melanie, Fatih and Shane work at the same … … disco / company.
2. It's … … Fatih's / Melanie's / Shane's / Natalie's idea to go to the disco.
3. Natalie can go to the disco … … on Wednesdays / only at the weekend.
4. Shane doesn't want to … … take the bus / go to the disco.
5. Fatih's parents think that the disco … … is great / isn't a good place.
6. Shane … … often / sometimes / never goes out in the evening.
7. Fatih *invites* the others to … … his flat for dinner / cook something.
8. Natalie will bring … … bread / blinis … … on Friday.

2 Look at the two *recipes* for meatballs.

Köfte (Turkish)

500 g	Rinderhackfleisch
200 g	gekochter Reis
2	Zwiebeln, gewürfelt
1	Bund Dill
je 1 TL	Pfeffer, Koriander, Salz, Piment, Thymian
4	Eier
1/8 l	Olivenöl
2 EL	Mehl

Rinderhackfleisch, Zwiebeln, Salz, Pfeffer, Koriander, Piment, Thymian, Dill, gekochten Reis und 1 Ei vermischen. Flache Klöße formen. In Mehl wenden und in verquirlte Eier tauchen. Olivenöl erhitzen und Hackfleischfladen von beiden Seiten goldbraun braten.

***Porcupine* meatballs** (American)

1 *lb ground beef*
½ cup *breadcrumbs*
1 *egg*
¾ *teaspoon salt*
¼ teaspoon paprika
¼ cup *raw rice*
6 cups tomato *sauce*

Mix ground beef, breadcrumbs, egg, salt and paprika. *Roll* into *flat* meatballs. Roll in ¼ cup raw rice. *Heat* tomato sauce in a *pot*. *Add* the meatballs. *Simmer* for 45 minutes. *Check seasoning*.

A **What is in the recipes? Tick what you need for each.**
Welche Zutaten braucht man für die Rezepte? Kreuzen Sie an.

	ground beef	*onions*	salt	egg(s)	bread	rice	tomato
Turkish	☐	☐	☐	☐	☐	☐	☐
American	☐	☐	☐	☐	☐	☐	☐

B **Translate the American recipe into German.**
Übersetzen Sie das amerikanische Rezept ins Deutsche.

to invite einladen
recipe (Koch-)Rezept
porcupine Stachelschwein
lb Abkürzung für Pfund (453,6 g)
ground beef Rinderhackfleisch
breadcrumbs Paniermehl
egg Ei
teaspoon Teelöffel
salt Salz
raw ungekocht
rice Reis
sauce Soße
to mix vermischen
to roll rollen
flat flach
to heat erhitzen
pot Topf
to add hinzufügen
to simmer köcheln
to check the seasoning abschmecken
onion Zwiebel

3 A **Look at the questionnaire below. Walk about the classroom. Ask questions like** *Have you been to the USA?*
Write down your classmate's name if the answer is *Yes, I have.* **Take turns to ask and answer.**
Stellen Sie Fragen wie im Beispiel. Bei positiven Antworten notieren Sie den Namen. Fragen und antworten Sie abwechselnd.

Find someone who ...	name
has been on TV. ►	
has met a famous person. ►	
has been to Italy. ►	
has had a car accident. ►	
has cooked a meal for the family. ►	
has been to a rock festival. ►	
has lived in another country. ►	
has been in hospital. ►	
has taken his / her driving test. ►	
has been in the newspaper. ►	

B **Report your answers.**
Berichten Sie, was Sie herausgefunden haben.

Examples: (Anna) has been to the USA.
Nobody has been on TV.

4 A **Put the verbs in brackets into present perfect.**
Setzen Sie die Verben ins present perfect.

Faruk (1. come) has come to Germany from *Africa*. He and his family (2. not be) haven't been here for long. They (3. live) ______ in a few German cities. He (4. find) ______ that it is very important to learn German *as* quickly *as possible*. Some people (5. not *accept*) ______ him because he doesn't speak good German. Faruk finds that difficult to understand. He (6. meet) ______ so many interesting people who can't speak German. People (7. not live) ______ on this planet for *hundreds* of years – they (8. live) ______ here much longer. They (9. speak) ______ hundreds of *languages*. They (10. do) ______ business together, (11. travel) ______ around the *world*. Of course, it (12. not be) ______ always ______ easy. Faruk wishes the Germans would be a bit more tolerant of people who (13. not learn) ______ to speak German perfectly.

Africa	Afrika	**to accept**	akzeptieren	**world**	Welt
as ... as	so ... wie	**hundreds**	Hunderte		
possible	möglich	**language**	Sprache		

B **Answer the following questions. Use short answers.**
Beantworten Sie die Fragen. Benutzen Sie die Kurzformen.

Examples: **Yes, he has. / No, he hasn't.**

1. Has Faruk found that learning German quickly is important?
2. Has he come to Germany from Italy?
3. Have all the people in Germany accepted him?
4. Has Faruk lived in more than one city in Germany?
5. Has Faruk been here for long?
6. Has he met many interesting people who don't speak German?
7. Have people lived on this planet for a short time?

5 **This is an interview with Hüsnü Çelebi, who lives in Germany. Write the interviewer's questions.**
Schreiben Sie die Fragen des Interviewers auf.

Interviewer: **Have you been in Germany for a long time?**
Hüsnü: I have been here for 15 years.
Interviewer: ______
Hüsnü: No, I haven't found anything difficult. When I'm friendly, people are friendly, too.
Interviewer: ______
Hüsnü: Yes, I have asked for a German *passport*.
Interviewer: ______
Hüsnü: Yes, I have often visited *Turkey*. I like the *relaxed* life there.
Interviewer: ______
Hüsnü: No, I have never wanted to live in Turkey.

passport Reisepass **Turkey** Türkei **relaxed** locker

Present perfect simple vollendete Gegenwart

(verneinte) Aussage: have / has (haven't / hasn't) + 3. Form

Positive Aussage	Verneinung	Frage
I have asked for a German passport.	**I haven't met** a TV star.	**Have I been** to Dublin?
You have been in Germany for a year.	**You haven't been** to France.	**Have you done** your homework?
He / she / it has found many friends.	**He / she / it hasn't found** a job.	**Has he / she / it rung** you?
We have had some problems.	**We haven't travelled** to Rome.	**Have we been** here long?
You have travelled to Italy.	**You haven't been** in hospital.	**Have you met** his parents?
They have accepted him.	**They haven't made** a meal.	**Have they been** to Turkey?

Anwendung

Have you tried the meatballs yet? Have you ever been to Berlin? I have never met a famous person. We haven't seen him since January.	mit bestimmten Adverbien z. B. yet / already, ever / never, since / for / How long …?
I have bought a car.	bei Handlungen ohne Zeitangabe

6 A Josie Day from California has sent an email to her German penfriend, Daniel. Read her email. When does she take her exams?
Josie Day aus Kalifornien hat ein E-Mail an ihren deutschen Brieffreund Daniel geschickt. Lesen Sie Josies E-Mail. Wann macht sie ihre Prüfungen?

From: Josie Day <josday@cool.us> To: Daniel Fischer <danielfischer@cool.us> Date: 04-03

Hi Daniel, As you can see I now have a computer. The best thing is *surfing* the internet. A few days ago I found a *web site* about school in Germany. It was really interesting – and very different from our school day. We finish at 3.15 p.m.; then team *practices* and clubs begin, for example German Club, Computer Club, band, *cheerleading*. That's a lot of fun!
We have four *quarters* in a school year – and in math and English we have to do an exam at the end of every quarter! I think the class tests in Germany are a better idea. It's very good that you have to learn languages in Germany. *Spanish* or German should be a *required course* at our school so that everybody has to take the *subject*. But they are only *electives*: you can choose if you want to take the subject.
Do you have a computer at home? Or do I still have to use the email address of your school? If you can't send an email, please write soon.
All the best, Josie

B Listen to the CD. Look at the words below and number them.
Hören Sie die CD. Sehen Sie sich die Wörter in Lautschrift an. Nummerieren Sie sie in der Reihenfolge wie auf der CD.

☐ [sɜːf] ______
☐ ['tʃɪəˌliːdɪŋ] ______
☐ ['sʌbdʒekt] ______
☐ ['spænɪʃ] ______
☐ [ɪ'lektɪv] ______
☐ ['kwɔːtə] ______
☐ [rɪ'kwaɪəd] ______
☐ ['præktɪs] ______
☐ ['webˌsaɪt] ______

C Listen to the CD again. Write the words next to the phonetic symbols in 6B.
Hören Sie die CD noch einmal. Schreiben Sie die Wörter neben die Lautschrift in **6B**.

D Write Daniel's answer (email or letter) to Josie. Imagine what he likes about school in America / in Germany.
Schreiben Sie Daniels Antwort (Brief oder E-Mail). Stellen Sie sich vor, was er wohl am jeweiligen Schulsystem gut findet.

7 PROJECT
Make a homepage in English for your school. Decide what you want to write about (sports, activities, a class trip).
Stellen Sie eine Seite (Homepage) auf Englisch für Ihre Schule zusammen. Entscheiden Sie, worüber Sie schreiben möchten (Sport, Aktivitäten, eine Klassenfahrt).

to surf	surfen	**quarter**	Schulsemester	**subject**	Fach
web site	Webseite	**Spanish**	Spanisch	**elective**	Wahlfach
practice	Übung; Training	**required course**	Pflichtfach		

Lifestyles 8

The *United Kingdom* and the *Republic* of Ireland are the two most important English-speaking countries in *Europe*. England, *Scotland, Wales* and *Northern* Ireland, which are parts of the United Kingdom, are also called 'countries'.

SCOTLAND
England is *south* of this country.

ENGLAND
This is the biggest and *best-known* country in the United Kingdom. London is its most important city.

NORTHERN IRELAND
This is *north* of the Republic of Ireland and it is part of the UK.

REPUBLIC OF IRELAND
This country is *west* of *Great Britain*. It is very large.

WALES
This is the smallest of the three countries on the island of Great Britain. It is west of England.

A **Read the texts above. Write down the names of the countries.**
Lesen Sie die Texte. Schreiben Sie die Ländernamen auf.

1. ______________________
2. ______________________
3. ______________________
4. ______________________
5. ______________________

B **What do you know about these places? Tell your classmates.**
Was wissen Sie über diese Länder? Erzählen Sie darüber.

Example: **England is famous for its football players.**

United Kingdom (UK) Vereinigtes Königreich	**Wales** Wales	**Great Britain** Großbritannien
republic Republik	**northern** Nord-	**south** südlich
Europe Europa	**north** nördlich	**east** östlich
Scotland Schottland	**best-known** bekannteste	
	west westlich	

1 Young people in Germany and Britain

Jamie Robertson is at a German college on an *exchange* trip. Edith Bensmann is interviewing him.

Edith: Jamie, could you tell us where you are from?

Jamie: I'm from Aberdeen in the northeast of Scotland. Aberdeen is an important *fishing port* and a university town.

Edith: You have been to Germany before. … Is life in Germany very different from life in the UK?

Jamie: No, not really. Of course, the language is different – and the food! German food's a bit better, and German *jokes* are a bit easier to understand. But there are still lots of things that are the same: Germans and *Brits* love football and *motor racing*, for example. And in the UK lots of young people go to *vocational* colleges, too, I think.

Edith: Hm – You talked about language and food but what other things are different?

Jamie: Well, I don't think that the *differences* are so great. Okay, we know that the Germans make *world-class* cars and that the British are *trendsetters* in fashion, hairstyles and music. But the important things in life, like friends and having *fun*, are the same in any country. And … we all worry about the same things – jobs and the future.

Edith: So, would you say that more is the same than is different?

Jamie: Yes, I would.

A **Match the photos with suitable words from the text. Write down the words below.**
Finden Sie für die Fotos die passenden Begriffe im Text. Schreiben Sie sie unten auf.

1. ______________________
2. ______________________
3. ______________________

B **The following words from the text have been split. Draw lines to show which parts belong together.**
Die Wörter aus dem Text sind getrennt worden. Verbinden Sie die richtigen Teile.

1. vocational
2. exchange
3. university
4. hair
5. motor
6. trend
7. fishing

setters | port | racing | college | town | styles | trip

1. vocational college
2. ______________________
3. ______________________
4. ______________________
5. ______________________
6. ______________________
7. ______________________

exchange Austausch	**Brit** Brite, Britin	**world-class** Weltklasse
fishing Fischerei	**motor racing** Autorennen	**trendsetter** Trendsetter
port Hafen	**vocational** Berufs-, beruflich	**fun** Spaß
joke Witz	**difference** Unterschied	

C **Look at the text in 1 again. Decide if Jamie said it or not. Put a ✗ in the correct box.**
Schauen Sie sich den Text in 1 noch einmal an. Hat Jamie das so oder ähnlich gesagt oder nicht? Kreuzen Sie an.

	Jamie said it.	He didn't say it.
1. English food is not as good as German food.	☐	☐
2. The British drink a lot of tea.	☐	✗
3. The British are leaders in hairstyles.	☐	☐
4. The British drive on the left.	☐	☐
5. English jokes are difficult to understand.	☐	☐
6. The Germans have *excellent* cars.	☐	☐

D **Find the opposites to the words in 1 – 6.**
Suchen Sie das Gegenteil zu den Wörtern in 1 – 6.

1. good	**a)** hot
2. big	**b)** difficult
3. old	**c)** late
4. cold	**d)** bad
5. early	**e)** small
6. easy	**f)** new

E **Write down the correct forms of the adjectives.**
Schreiben Sie die richtigen Steigerungsformen der Adjektive auf.

1. old	older	oldest
2. cold		
3.		latest
4.	hotter	
5.		biggest
6.	easier	
7.	better	
8. bad		worst
9.		most difficult

F **Write the adjectives in the correct form.**
Vervollständigen Sie die Sätze. Benutzen Sie die richtige Form des Adjektivs.

1. Some people say that German food is (good) better than English food.

2. London is (big) ____________ than Berlin, but it is not the (big) ____________ city in the world.

3. German jokes are (easy) ____________ to understand than English jokes.

4. Jamie thinks that the German language is (difficult) ____________ than English.

excellent ausgezeichnet

2 Edith was interested in the exchange programme. So she went to Aberdeen. This is part of her *diary* about life with Jamie's family.

When Jamie and Adrian were small, the Robertsons woke up cheerfully on Saturday mornings because there was no school and no job to go to. They drank their tea happily in bed and had lots of time. Now everything is different. Jamie and Adrian have a cup of coffee and some toast or cereal. At 8 o'clock they leave the house quickly. They have no time because they work at a DIY centre regularly after college and on Saturdays. Pete, their father, makes the tea and some toast in the kitchen. Janet (that's Mrs Robertson) carries the bottles of milk carefully into the house. The milkman does not only deliver milk, he also brings other things like yoghurt and cream.

A **Unscramble the sentences about the Robertsons.**
Bringen Sie die Wörter in die richtige Reihenfolge.

1. some / for breakfast / they / cereal / have / toast or
   They have some toast or cereal for breakfast.
2. in the kitchen / the / he / tea / makes
3. work / a DIY centre / on Saturdays / at / they
4. milk / the / and / delivers / other things / milkman
5. coffee / they / in the morning / a cup of / have

B **Underline the adverbs in Edith's diary.**
Unterstreichen Sie die Adverbien in Ediths Tagebuch.

C **Write down the adverbs you have found. Fill in the adjective forms.**
Schreiben Sie die Adverbien auf, die Sie gefunden haben.
Vervollständigen Sie die Tabelle mit den Adjektiv-Formen.

	adverb	adjective
1.	cheerfully	cheerful
2.		
3.		
4.		
5.		

diary Tagebuch
cheerful(ly) fröhlich
cereal Frühstücksgetreide
DIY (Do It Yourself) Heimwerker-
regular(ly) regelmäßig
milkman Milchmann
to deliver liefern

3 **How do the following people do their jobs? Use the verbs and adverbs in their correct forms.**
Wie machen folgende Leute ihren Job? Benutzen Sie die Verben und Adverbien in ihrer richtigen Form.

Examples: **A detective works carefully.**
A taxi driver drives his taxi well.

A	shop assistant builder football player taxi driver reporter painter car mechanic secretary pop star	plays works drives writes paints speaks	(…)	beautiful careful easy slow professional good	(…)

I Word order Wortstellung

(In the morning)	Pete	makes	tea	in the kitchen	(in the morning).
Zeit	Subjekt	Verb	Objekt	Ort	Zeit

Die grundsätzliche Wortstellung im Englischen ist **S – V – O** (Subjekt – Verb – Objekt). Adverbien des Ortes folgen dem Objekt. Adverbien der Zeit stehen ganz am Anfang oder ganz am Ende des Satzes.

II Adverbs Adverbien

Adjective	Adverb	
careful	carefully	Das Adverb wird aus Adjektiv und -ly gebildet.
happy	happ**ily**	-y wird zu -ily
good	well	Einige Adverbien bilden unregelmäßige Formen.

Anwendung

The reporter writes professionally. — Adverbien werden benutzt um auszudrücken, wie man etwas tut.

III Comparison of adjectives Steigerung von Eigenschaftswörtern

old	older	oldest	Steigerung der kurzen Adjektive mit -er und -est
easy	easier	easiest	-y wird zu -ier und -iest
big	bigger	biggest	nach kurzen Vokalen wird der Endkonsonant verdoppelt
good	better	best	einige Adjektive haben unregelmäßige Steigerungsformen
difficult	more difficult	most difficult	längere Adjektive werden mit more und most gesteigert

Anwendung

London is bigger than Berlin. — Komparativsätze werden mit … than gebildet.

4 Mrs Robertson's sister Lucy is talking to her *husband*, Will. They have just got an *invitation* to the birthday party of their nephew, Jamie, who will be eighteen on Thursday.

A **Listen to the text. What would Jamie like for his birthday?**
Hören Sie die CD. Was möchte Jamie zum Geburtstag haben?

B **Look at the pictures and tick the ones that you have heard in the text.**
Schauen Sie sich die Abbildungen an. Kreuzen Sie die an, von denen gesprochen wurde.

1 ○

2 ○

3 ○

4 ○

5 ○

6 ○

C **Listen to the CD again. Tick 'true' or 'false'.**
Hören Sie den Dialog noch einmal. Kreuzen Sie an.

	true	false
1. Lucy says that eighteen-year-olds listen to older people.	☐	☐
2. A driving licence *means* that young people feel *free*.	☒	☐
3. Some parents are happy when they don't have to drive their kids.	☐	☐
4. All young Brits buy their cars.	☐	☐
5. Some accidents happen when young people drive too fast.	☐	☐
6. Parents can teach their children to drive in the United Kingdom.	☐	☐
7. In Britain people don't have to take a driving test.	☐	☐

5 **Role play: A family discussion.**
Is it really *necessary* to get a driving licence (at eighteen)?
Prepare a list of *typical* arguments for the positions of parents who say 'no' and for young people who say 'yes'.

Copy the arguments onto role cards, then play the roles.
Schreiben Sie die Argumente auf Karten. Spielen Sie dann die Rollen.

to agree with someone
Yes, you're right.
Yes, that's very true.
That's how I feel, too.

to disagree with someone
I'm not sure about that.
I can't agree with you.
I don't think that's right.

husband Ehemann
invitation Einladung
to mean bedeuten
free frei
to believe glauben
anyone (irgend)jemand
speed limit Geschwindigkeitbegrenzung
guardian angel Schutzengel
costs Kosten
to fetch (ab)holen
necessary nötig
typical typisch

Town and country 9

Hillford
How an *artist* saw the town 25 years ago.

A **Look at the drawing and find the things in the box. Write the names down below.**
Schauen Sie die Zeichnung an. Schreiben Sie die Wörter aus dem Kasten an die richtige Stelle.

cars	houses	river
station	train	disco
cinema	smoke	

1 factory
2
3 hill
4
5
6
7
8
9
10
11
12
13 bridge
14

B **Look at the boxes and make sentences. Say where each thing is in the picture above.**
Schauen Sie die Dinge auf dem Bild oben an. Beschreiben Sie, wo etwas ist. Fangen Sie so an:

Examples: In the picture you can see / find …
there is / are …
the … is …

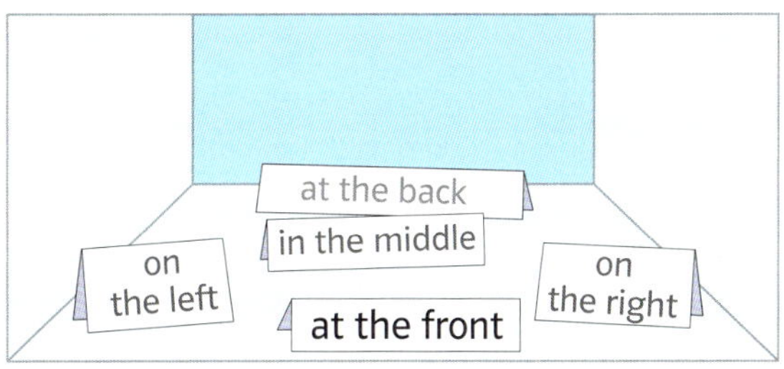

artist Künstler/in
factory Fabrik
hill Hügel
plane Flugzeug
lorry LKW, Lastwagen
bridge Brücke
traffic lights Verkehrsampel
at the back hinten
in the middle in der Mitte, mitten in
at the front vorne

1 The *cucumber* kids

Many people think that big cities are *dirty* and *dangerous*. There is too much crime and the air is *polluted*. There are also a lot of poor people who don't have jobs. In Detroit, USA, some people have found a way to make city life greener and safer: They are making gardens. They call themselves the 'gardening angels' and they have *already* made over 200 gardens, in the middle of the poorest *areas*!

At first the 'gardening angels' were a group of older people. Later, some of their gardens, often next to drug *dealers'* houses, *attracted* the *local* kids. The dealers even *moved out* of one house – they and their *customers* hated the *smell* of the *compost*. "The other kids were *impressed* by that," says one of the 'angels'. "They thought these dealers were so big and hard, and we *got rid of* them.

The kids started to help us in the garden. We called them the 'cucumber kids' because they liked to eat the cucumbers. Later, they sold their own *vegetables*. The first day they made $40 in three hours! That was the first time they saw a future!"

Now the 'angels' also give some of the food to people without homes or jobs. "It's a green *revolution*. We must find our own work and help to make a future for us and our city."

A Read the text "The cucumber kids" and find the opposites of the underlined words in the text.

Lesen Sie den Text und finden Sie jeweils das Gegenteil der unterstrichenen Wörter im Text.

1. Detroit is not a <u>small</u> town, it is a b__________ city.
2. The streets are often not <u>clean</u>, they are d__________ and p__________ .
3. There is a lot of crime in some streets, so it is not very <u>safe</u> there, it is d__________ .
4. Dealers <u>buy</u> drugs and s__________ them to their customers.
5. First <u>older people</u> started to make gardens, now also k__________ help them.

B Match the sentences below to the people who said them.

Ordnen Sie die Sätze unten den Leuten zu, die sie gesagt haben.

1. What a smell!
2. Can we help you in your garden?
3. Let's make a garden here.
4. Wow, we've made so much money already!
5. Let's move to another area.
6. Let's put more compost on the garden.
7. Can we have some cucumbers, please?
8. We could give some food to people without homes!
9. Listen, kid! I'm the boss round here.

gardening angels:	3		
cucumber kids:			
drug dealers:			

cucumber	Salatgurke	**area**	Gegend	**smell**	Geruch
dirty	schmutzig	**dealer**	Händler/in, Dealer	**compost**	Kompost
dangerous	gefährlich	**to attract**	anziehen	**to impress**	beeindrucken
to pollute	(Umwelt) verschmutzen	**local**	aus der Gegend, örtlich	**to get rid of**	loswerden
		to move out	aus-, wegziehen	**vegetable**	Gemüse
already	schon	**customer**	Kunde, Kundin	**revolution**	Revolution

C **Complete the sentences with information from the text in 1.**
Vervollständigen Sie die Sätze mit den Informationen aus dem Text in **1**.

1. People often don't like cities because ______________________ .
2. The 'gardening angels' started to make gardens because ______________________ .
3. The smell of the compost was so bad that ______________________ .
4. The other kids were impressed because ______________________ .
5. The kids liked to eat cucumbers so ______________________ .

D **Find the following words in the text.**
Suchen Sie die folgenden Wörter im Text.

1. People who buy and sell drugs: ______________________ .
2. Something you use in a garden so that things *grow* better: ______________________ .
3. Long, green vegetables: ______________________ .
4. People who do not have very much money: ______________________ .
5. Things like *carrots* and *potatoes*: ______________________ .
6. When something is not clean: ______________________ .

2 **The following signs in a park in Detroit help to keep the city clean and safe. They tell people what to do or not to do. Fill in the gaps with 'must', 'must not', 'can' and 'need not'.**
Die folgenden Schilder in einem Park in Detroit helfen, die Stadt sauber und sicher zu machen. Vervollständigen Sie die Sätze mit **'must', 'must not', 'can' and 'need not'.**

1. People ______________ park their cars here.
2. You ______________ keep the picnic area clean.
3. You ______________ ride your bike on the grass.
4. You ______________ keep your dog on a *lead* here.
5. You ______________ smoke here.
6. Children ______________ play in this area.
7. People ______________ bring their *own* food and drinks,
   but they ______________ bring their own tables and chairs.

to grow	wachsen	**potato**	Kartoffel	**own**	eigene(r)
carrot	Karotte	**lead**	Leine		

3 Anna lives in the country. Her cousin Jessica is from London.
Jessica wants to know all about life in the country.

A **Match Anna's answers to Jessica's questions.**
Ordnen Sie die Fragen und Antworten zu.

Jessica: **1.** Do many / a lot of people visit you?
2. Do you go to many / a lot of parties?
3. How much time do you spend at home?
4. Is there much to do in the evenings?

Anna: **a)** Well, you can visit friends, go to the disco or watch TV.
b) Not much really. I'm at college all day and out at the weekend.
c) Not to many, but usually to one a week.
d) Oh yes, a lot of my friends come, or I go and see them.

1.	d)
2.	
3.	
4.	

B **Anna asks Jessica about her life in London. Complete the sentences with 'much', 'many' or 'a lot of'.**
Vervollständigen Sie die Sätze mit **much**, **many** oder **a lot of**.

1. How ______________ time does it take to get to your college?

2. Quite ______________ time really, about one and a half hours.

3. And are there always ______________ people on the trains?

4. Yes, there's often not ______________ room to sit down.

5. And how ______________ does it cost?

6. Quite ______________ money.

7. What about going out? How ______________ evenings a week do you go out?

8. That's hard to say! It's often a question of how ______________ money I've got.

9. Cities are such *noisy* places – is there ______________ *noise* where you live?

10. Well, I live near a *main* road so there are ______________ cars
and ______________ noise during the day. But London is great –
it has so much to *offer*, I love this city!

4 **While Jessica is staying with Anna, they decide to have a party.**
Jessica makes a list of things to check before the party.

food		**drink**		**other**	
crisps ✓	tomatoes	cola ✓	coffee ✓	paper cups	knives ✓
peanuts	cheese ✓	orange juice	tea ✓	glasses ✓	forks ✓
bread rolls	salad	water ✓	milk	paper plates	spoons ✓

noisy laut
noise Lärm, Krach
main Haupt-
to offer (an-)bieten
crisps (Kartoffel-)Chips
peanut Erdnuss
bread roll kleines weiches Brötchen
salad (angemachter) Salat
orange juice Orangensaft
plate Teller
knife, knives Messer
fork Gabel
spoon Löffel

Jessica talks to Anna about her list. Read their conversation, then complete the sentences with 'some' or 'any'.
Sie geht mit Anna die Liste durch. Lesen Sie die Unterhaltung der beiden. Vervollständigen Sie die Sätze mit **some** oder **any.**

1. Anna, have you got __any__ crisps for the party tomorrow?
2. Yes, I think we've got __some__ but I'll have to check.
3. What about peanuts?
4. Oh, we haven't got __any__ peanuts. We'll have to get some later.
5. I think we'll need __some__ bread rolls.
6. Yes, good idea, we'll get ______ tomorrow.
7. I think we'll need ______ salad.
8. I haven't got ______ salad, we'll get ______ tomorrow.
9. Have you got ______ ?
10. Yes, I think there is ______ .

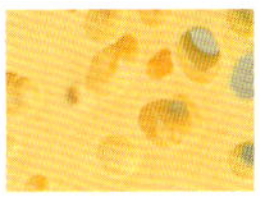

11. I think we'll need ______ .
12. I haven't got ______ .

Quantifiers   Mengenangaben

► **much / a lot of – viel;   many / a lot of – viele**

Anwendung

There's a lot of pollution in cities. There are a lot of cars on the streets.	In bejahten Sätzen wird 'a lot of' bevorzugt.
There isn't a lot of / much sugar. There aren't a lot of / many spoons. Are there a lot of / many glasses?	In verneinten Sätzen bzw. Fragen kann man beide Formen gebrauchen.
How much time do you spend at home? How many people have you invited?	Nach 'how' müssen 'much' oder 'many' stehen.

► **some / any**

Anwendung

We need some coffee / tomatoes.	In bejahten Aussagesätzen wird some verwendet.
Have you got any cheese / plates? We haven't got any tea / juice.	In Fragen oder verneinten Aussagesätzen wird any benutzt.

Modal auxiliaries   Hilfsverben

You	can	go home after college.	können, dürfen
You	must	write tests at college.	müssen
You	must not (mustn't)	listen to music in class.	nicht dürfen
You	need not (needn't)	pay for college.	nicht brauchen / nicht müssen

5 A Two young people are talking about how they live. Listen to the CD. Who lives in California?
Zwei junge Leute sprechen darüber, wie sie leben. Hören Sie die CD. Wer lebt in Kalifornien?

B Listen again and fill in the chart below.
Hören Sie die CD noch einmal. Vervollständigen Sie die Tabelle.

What are their names? ►		
Who do they live with? ►		
Where do they live now? ►		
Where did they live before? ►		
Why did they move? ►		
What do they like about the country? ►		
What do they miss? ►		

C Write a short paragraph about one of the two people. Use the information from 5B.
Schreiben Sie einen kurzen Text über eine der beiden Personen. Benutzen Sie die Informationen aus **5B**.

6 Mr Jackson's farm near Hobart. Look at the map and read the text. Work out what all the symbols on the map mean. Complete the key.
Schauen Sie sich die Karte an und lesen Sie den Text. Was bedeuten die Symbole auf der Karte? Vervollständigen Sie die Erklärungen.

Mr Jackson is a farmer. A *railway* runs across his farm. Three quarters of the farm is grassland for *cows*. The rest of the farm *produces* apples, *except* for a small vegetable garden near the house. Mr Jackson *grows* tomatoes in it.

He and his family go shopping in Hobart. All the shops are near the church.

Mr Jackson has two children: the oldest works in a large factory in Hobart near the railway. His daughter is still at school. Her school is called Hobart Junior High.

glad	froh	**nature**	Natur	**except**	außer
to save	sparen	**railway**	Bahnlinie	**to grow**	anpflanzen
apartment	(US) Wohnung	**cow**	Kuh	**church**	Kirche
simple	einfach	**to produce**	produzieren		

Travelling in Europe

10

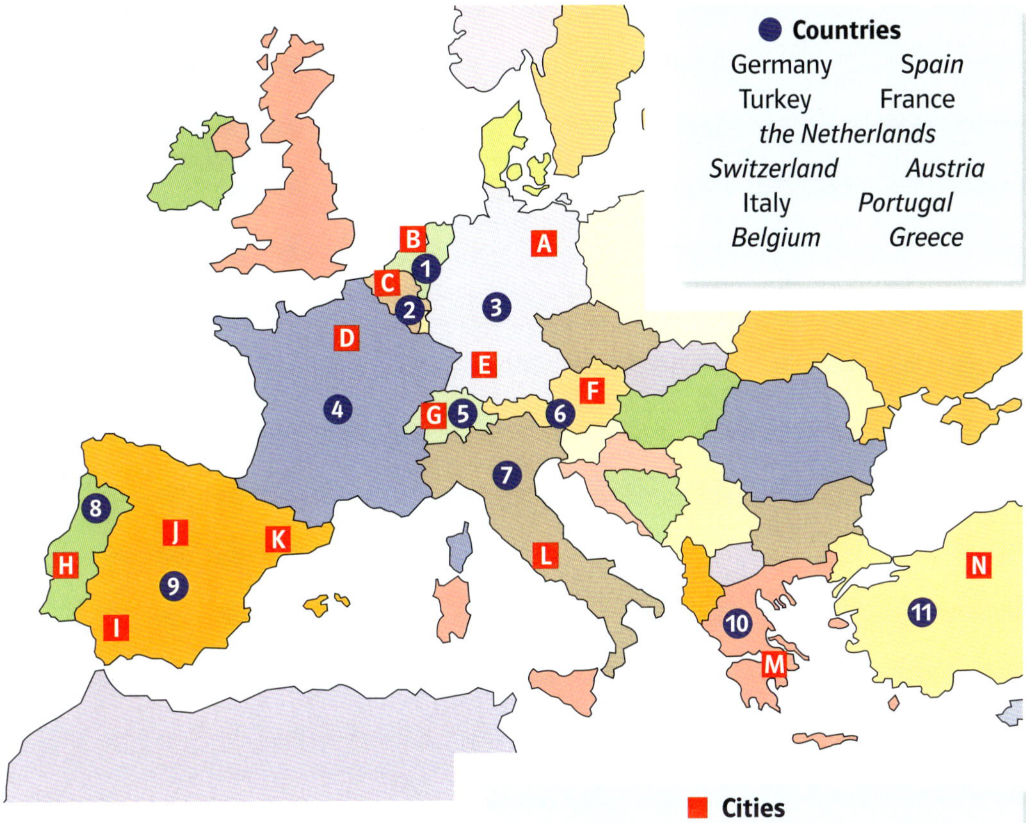

Countries

Germany *Spain*
Turkey France
the Netherlands
Switzerland *Austria*
Italy *Portugal*
Belgium *Greece*

Cities

Amsterdam Barcelona Ankara
Berlin Paris Seville Vienna
Stuttgart Athens Rome Brussels
Berne Lisbon Madrid

A **Work with your partner. Write down the names of the countries and cities.**
Partnerarbeit. Schreiben Sie die Namen der Länder und Städte auf.

B **Three of the cities in the box are not the *capitals* of their countries. Which are they? Write them down.**
Drei der Städte im Kasten sind nicht Hauptstadt ihres Landes. Welche sind das? Schreiben Sie sie auf.

C **Look at the map. You want to travel from Berlin to Barcelona and Lisbon by train. Which countries do you go through?**
Schauen Sie auf die Karte. Sie wollen mit dem Zug von Berlin über Barcelona nach Lissabon fahren. Durch welche Länder fahren Sie?

Spain	Spanien	**Switzerland**	die Schweiz	**Belgium**	Belgien
the Netherlands	die Niederlande	**Austria**	Österreich	**Greece**	Griechenland
		Portugal	Portugal	**capital**	Hauptstadt

1

It was summer in Spain. Emrel, 19, a young Turkish man, was on an *InterRail* trip to Barcelona. On the train he met two girls.

Emrel: Hi, are you on holiday, too?
Anne: Yes, we are on a three-week holiday and are travelling round Spain and Portugal.
Emrel: Are you enjoying your trip?
Anne: Yes, very much. And *most of all*, it isn't too *expensive*. We bought an InterRail ticket before we started. *By the way* – I'm Anne and this is my sister Linda. What's your name?
Emrel: I'm Emrel. Where are you going?
Linda: Well, we want to visit Barcelona first, then we'll travel to Seville. From there we'll go to Tavira in Portugal where we want to stay a little longer. We've read that there is a large *campsite* there – an insider tip for young people.
Emrel: Right. I was there last summer. Fantastic *weather*.
Anne: Did you enjoy staying there?
Emrel: Yeah, it was great. Nice place to stay longer. Lots of young people there. *It was real fun!*
Linda: *Sounds good!* By the way, Emrel – where are you from?
Emrel: Well, from Berlin, that's in Germany.
Anne: Oh no, that's ... das gibt's doch gar nicht!
Linda: Wir sind auch aus Deutschland. Wir kommen aus Stuttgart. Und wir reden die ganze Zeit Englisch miteinander!

A

Underline the correct statement.
Unterstreichen Sie die richtige Aussage.

1. Emrel is German / Spanish / Turkish.
2. Emrel lives in Berlin / Barcelona / Stuttgart.
3. Emrel is at work / on holiday.
4. Anne is a Turkish / a German / an English girl.
5. Linda is Anne's friend / mother / sister.
6. They are both from Berlin / Stuttgart / Seville.
7. The three young people are travelling by plane / car / train.
8. Anne and Linda's holiday lasts a few days / a few weeks / a week.
9. Barcelona is in Italy / Spain / Portugal.
10. Emrel was in Tavira two years ago / a year ago / a long time ago.

B

Find words in the text in 1 which have the same meaning as the following words or explanations.
Suchen Sie Wörter im Text in **1**, die dasselbe bedeuten wie folgende Wörter und Erklärungen.

1. country west of Spain ______________________
2. fantastic great ______________
3. many ______________________

InterRail	InterRail (Zugreisen zu Sonderkonditionen)	**expensive**	teuer	**It was real fun!**	Es hat echt Spaß gemacht!
most of all	am besten, am meisten	**by the way**	übrigens	**Sounds good!**	Hört sich gut an!
		campsite	Zeltplatz		
		weather	Wetter		

4. piece of paper that shows that you have paid the *fare* ____________
5. to go from place to place by train, plane, etc. ____________
6. a time when you don't have to work ____________

C **Find words with the opposite meaning in the text in 1.**
Suchen Sie Wörter mit gegenteiliger Bedeutung im Text in **1**.

1. small ____________
2. cheap ____________
3. shorter ____________
4. winter ____________
5. bad ____________
6. a lot ____________
7. sold bought
8. last ____________

D **Do you remember the following short statements in 1? Make complete sentences.**
Erinnern Sie sich an die folgenden kurzen Aussagen in **1**?
Schreiben Sie diese Aussagen als ganze Sätze auf.

1. Anne: Yes, very much. (line 7)
   Yes, we're enjoying it very much.
2. Emrel: Fantastic weather. (line ___)
   ____
3. Emrel: Right. (line ___)
   ____
4. Emrel: Lots of young people. (line ___)
   ____
5. Linda: Sounds good! (line ___)
   ____
6. Emrel: Well, from Berlin. (line ___)
   ____

2 **A** **Ask your partner the following questions. Write down his / her answers.**
Stellen Sie sich gegenseitig folgende Fragen. Schreiben Sie die Antworten auf.

1. Where did you spend your last holiday?
2. Did you go there with your parents, friends or anybody else?
3. How did you get there?
4. How long did you stay?
5. What is your *favourite* kind of holiday?

Examples:
1. I spent ... in ...
2. I went ...
3. I / We travelled by ...
4. I / We stayed for ...
5. My favourite ...

B **Report about your partner's last holiday.**
Berichten Sie, was Sie gegenseitig über Ihre letzten Ferien herausgefunden haben.

fare Fahrpreis **favourite** liebste/r/s

3 **Rewrite the sentences about young people's holiday activities. Use the verbs in brackets and a suitable -ing form.**
Schreiben Sie die Sätze über die Ferienaktivitäten noch einmal. Benutzen Sie die Verben in Klammern und eine passende **-ing** Form.

1. Anne: I often go to the disco in the evening. (like / go)
   Anne likes going to the disco in the evening.
2. Kerry: I sometimes watch TV, but more often I read. (*prefer* / read / watch)
   Kerry prefers reading to ...
3. Henry: I haven't had time to learn French *yet*. I'll do that in my next holidays. (start / learn)
   ____
4. Sally: I never do any housework in my holidays. I don't like that at all. (hate / do)
   ____
5. Darren: I go *fishing* as often as possible. It's my favourite hobby. (love / fish)
   ____
6. Diana: Water sports are my favourite holiday activities. (enjoy / *sail* / swim)
   ____
7. Derek: I smoke a lot. But I really want *to give* it *up* now. (stop / smoke)
   Derek wants to ...

4 **Fill in a suitable preposition from the box.**
Vervollständigen Sie den Text mit einer passenden Präposition aus dem Kasten.

without for of at
in about in after ~~on~~

Some tips (1) ________ travelling in London

Don't be afraid (2) ________ travelling to *such a* big city. Everybody will be helpful. But if you are bad (3) ________ driving in town centres, you shouldn't drive into London. And of course, you will have *difficulty* (4) ________ finding a parking space. You can buy 'The London parking guide' which gives you *useful* information (5) on parking in London. It is much easier to go by bus or underground. Do you want to save money? How (6) ________ buying your tourist ticket after 9.30 a.m.? *As* there is a lot of *traffic*, be careful when *crossing* the streets. Only cross (7) ________ looking right (!) first. If you are interested (8) ________ looking at the *sights*, you can't do it (9) ________ buying a London guide and map! And if you don't know how to get somewhere, ask one of the friendly policemen.

to prefer vorziehen
not ... yet noch nicht
fishing Angeln
sailing Segeln
to give up (smoking) (das Rauchen) aufgeben
such a solch ein/e/r
difficulty Schwierigkeit
useful nützlich
as da, weil
traffic Verkehr
to cross überqueren
sights Sehenswürdigkeiten

5 **A** **Fill in 'to' before the infinitive where necessary.**
Vervollständigen Sie die Sätze mit **to** wo nötig.

situation ►

1. You want ____ *book* a *seat*.
2. You don't like cigarette smoke.
3. You would like ____ travel *overnight*.
4. You are not able ____ walk.
5. You have decided ____ take your dog with you.
6. You need ____ change trains on your journey.
7. You are under 26.

tip ►

a) You can ____ make a *reservation* for a bed.
b) You must ____ book your seat at least two days before you want ____ travel.
c) Somebody will ____ help you at the station and on the train.
d) You should ____ book a *non-smoking* seat.
e) Don't forget ____ find out the *platform* number of the next train.
f) You are allowed ____ buy a Eurorail ticket.
g) You have ____ pay half price for your *pet*.

B **Match the situations with the right tips.**
Ordnen Sie die Situationen den richtigen Tipps zu.

1. b 2. ☐ 3. ☐ 4. ☐ 5. ☐ 6. ☐ 7. ☐

to book reservieren, buchen
seat (Sitz-)Platz
overnight über Nacht
reservation Reservierung
non-smoking Nichtraucher
platform Bahnsteig
pet Haustier

The gerund Das Gerundium (-ing Form)

Anwendung

Anne likes **going** to the disco.	nach bestimmten Verben, z. B. like, enjoy, love, hate, prefer, start, stop
Sarah is interested in **travelling** to Spain. The boy crossed the road without **looking**.	nach Präpositionen

The infinitive Der Infinitiv (die Grundform des Verbs)

Anwendung

ohne to	You should **travel** to Spain in June.	nach den meisten Hilfsverben, z. B. should, must, can, will
mit to	He wants **to stay** at home.	nach bestimmten Verben, z. B. want to, decide to, need to, have to, remember to, forget to, would like to, be allowed to, be able to

6 **Some *Australian* tourists are on a sightseeing tour of some famous cities in Europe. The guide gives them a lot of information about the cities.**

A **Listen to the CD. Write the names of the cities below the three pictures.**
Hören Sie die CD. Schreiben Sie die Namen der Städte unter die drei Bilder.

► ____________________

► ____________________

► ____________________

B **Listen again to the CD. Fill in the rest of the information.**
Hören Sie die CD noch einmal. Vervollständigen Sie die Tabelle.

city ►			
inhabitants ►			
sights ►			
further information ►			
evening programme ►			

C **Write a short report about one of the cities.**
Schreiben Sie einen kurzen Bericht über eine der Städte.

Australian	australisch	**lady**	Dame	**known**	bekannt
inhabitant	Einwohner/in	**gentleman**	Herr	**while**	während
to pass	vorbei fahren / gehen	**to be delighted**	sich freuen	**to arrange**	arrangieren

A normal day for DJ AC (*Absolutely* Cool)

A **Draw the hands of the clock in the circle.**
Zeichnen Sie die Uhrzeiger in den Kreisen.

1. At **10.00 a.m.** DJ AC gets up and has breakfast.

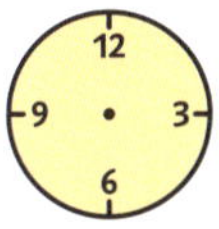

2. At **11.30 a.m.** he has a shower. He puts on his last clean t-shirt.

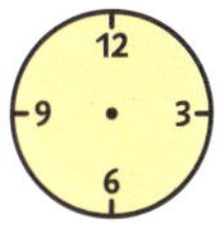

3. At **11.45 a.m.** DJ AC drives to a *launderette*.

4. At **1.15 a.m.** he phones a manager at a record company.

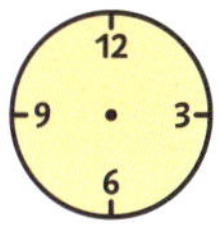

B **Read the sentences below and write down the times.**
Lesen Sie die Sätze unten und schreiben Sie die Uhrzeiten auf.

1. At **2.25 p.m.** he chooses songs for the evening. ______
2. At **3.08 p.m.** he has lunch in a Chinese restaurant. ______
3. At **3.45 p.m.** DJ AC has a short sleep at home. ______
4. At **4.30 p.m.** he takes the dog for a walk. ______
5. At **5.05 p.m.** he is home again and his friend Simon arrives. ______
6. Until **5.52 p.m.** the two friends talk about the day. ______

C **Write the correct times and draw the hands of the clock.**
Schreiben Sie die richtigen Uhrzeiten auf und zeichnen Sie die Uhrzeiger.

1. At (**6 p.m.**)
______
DJ AC watches the news on TV.

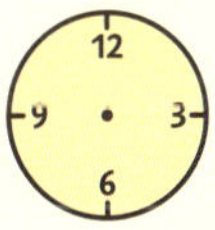

2. At (**7.55 p.m.**)
______
he arrives at the disco and starts work.

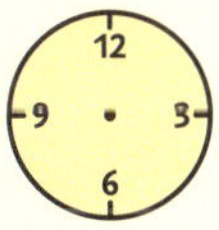

3. At (**12 p.m.**)
______
the young people dance and have fun.

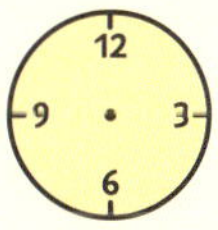

4. At (**2.35 a.m.**)
______
DJ AC goes home for supper.

absolutely absolut **launderette** Waschsalon **midnight** Mitternacht

A trip around England

A **Listen to the dialogue between Colin and Angie. Draw their honeymoon trip on the map. Start in Canterbury.**
Hören Sie den Dialog zwischen Colin und Angie an. Tragen Sie die Route ein, die sie in den Flitterwochen zurückgelegt haben. Fangen Sie in Canterbury an.

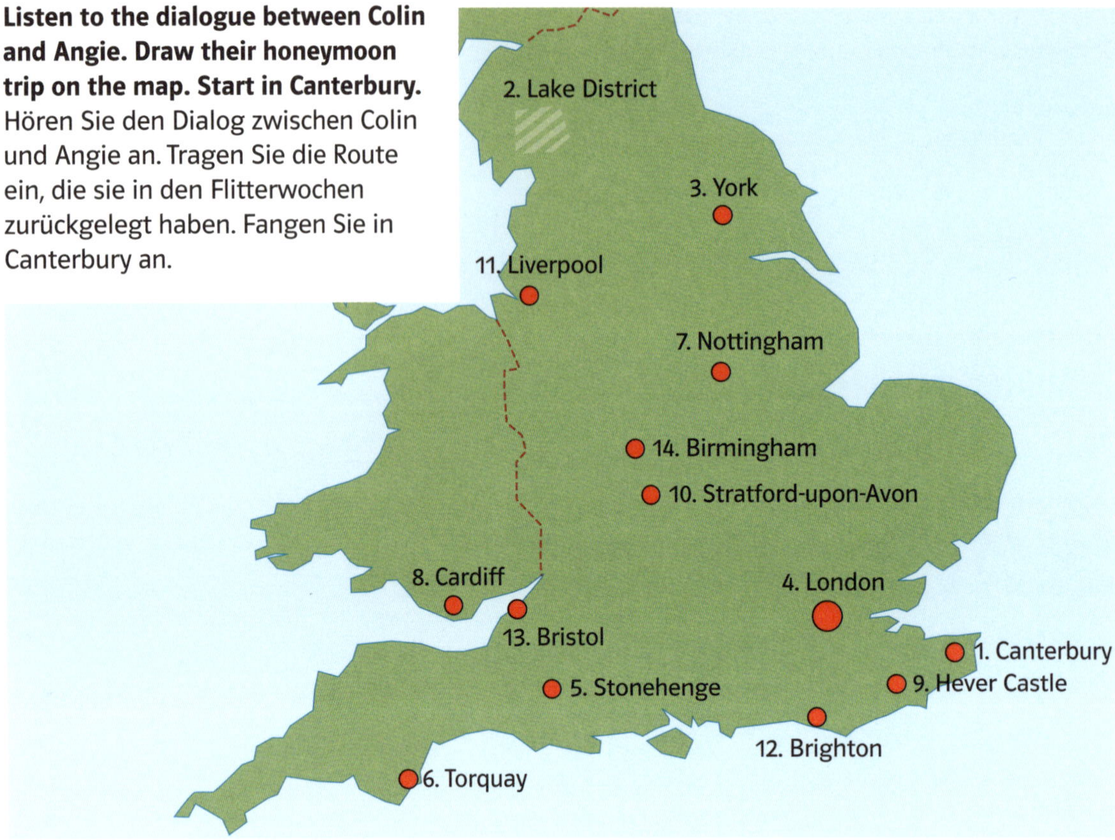

B **Listen to the CD again and look at the photos. Where did Angie and Colin take the photos below? Write down the correct number under the photos.**
Hören Sie den Dialog noch einmal an. Wo haben Colin and Angie die Fotos gemacht? Schreiben Sie die richtige Ziffer unter die Fotos.

a) ____

b) ____

c) ____

d) 1

e) ____

f) ____

Christmas in England

Match the words in 1–8 with the right pictures.
Ordnen Sie die Wörter 1–8 den Bildern zu.

I am Santa Claus. I have got the ideal job because I have to work only once a year in December. But then there is very much to do! It is a bit dangerous when I fly in the air with my (1.) **sleigh** but I have some good helpers. Their 'boss' is Rudolph with his (2.) **red nose**. He flies before all the other (3.) **reindeer**. On Christmas Eve I wait until all the children are asleep. Then I land on the (4.) **roof** and I *climb* down the (5.) **chimney**. Before I fill the children's stockings with sweets I drink a glass of milk and eat a piece of (6.) **Christmas pudding**. Then I put all of the (7.) **presents** which the children get on Christmas morning under the Christmas tree.
In a typical English house the living room is *decorated* with Christmas cards and (8.) **mistletoe**. Do you know a good *custom* in England? A young man has to kiss a young woman when they are standing under the mistletoe. I wear a long red coat and brown boots. I carry a large sack with all the sweets and presents that the children are waiting for.

a) ______________

b) ______________

c) ______________

d) ______________

e) ______________

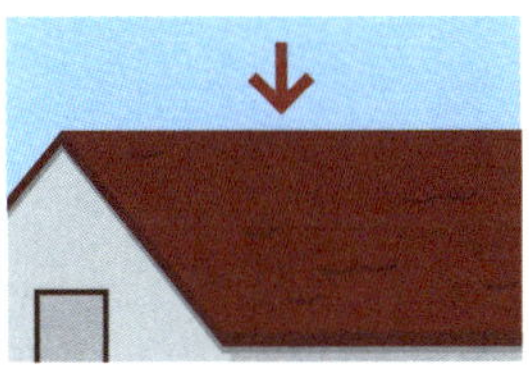
f) ______________

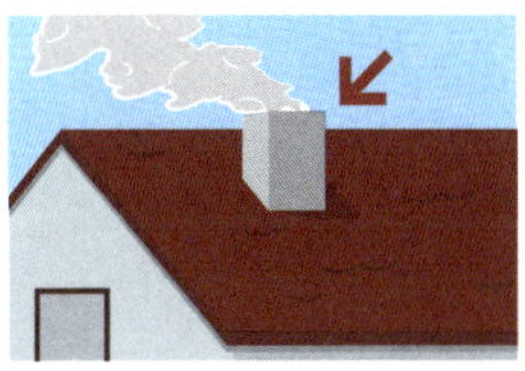
g) ______________

h) ______________

to climb klettern **to decorate** schmücken **custom** Brauch

Word order

A **Cut out the boxes. Put the words into the correct order.**
Schneiden Sie die Wörter aus. Setzen Sie die Wörter in die richtige Reihenfolge.

1.	normally	Girls	wear	clothes	modern	.	
2.	their homework	don't	always	.	Pupils	do	
3.	Jane	Where	?	go	to	does	on Mondays
4.	sitting	Kate	.	the sun	is	in	now
5.	When	leaving	school	the students	?	are	today
6.	this evening	visiting	friend	is	his	Tom	.
7.	Janina	at 8 o'clock	.	every day	to school	goes	
8.	today	carrying	her	Liz	umbrella	.	is	not

B **Make new sentences with the words.**
Bilden Sie neue Sätze mit den Wörtern.

Computers

11

In Germany we often use English words when we talk about computers. Name the parts of the multimedia computer. Use the words below.
Benennen Sie die Teile des Multimedia-Computers.

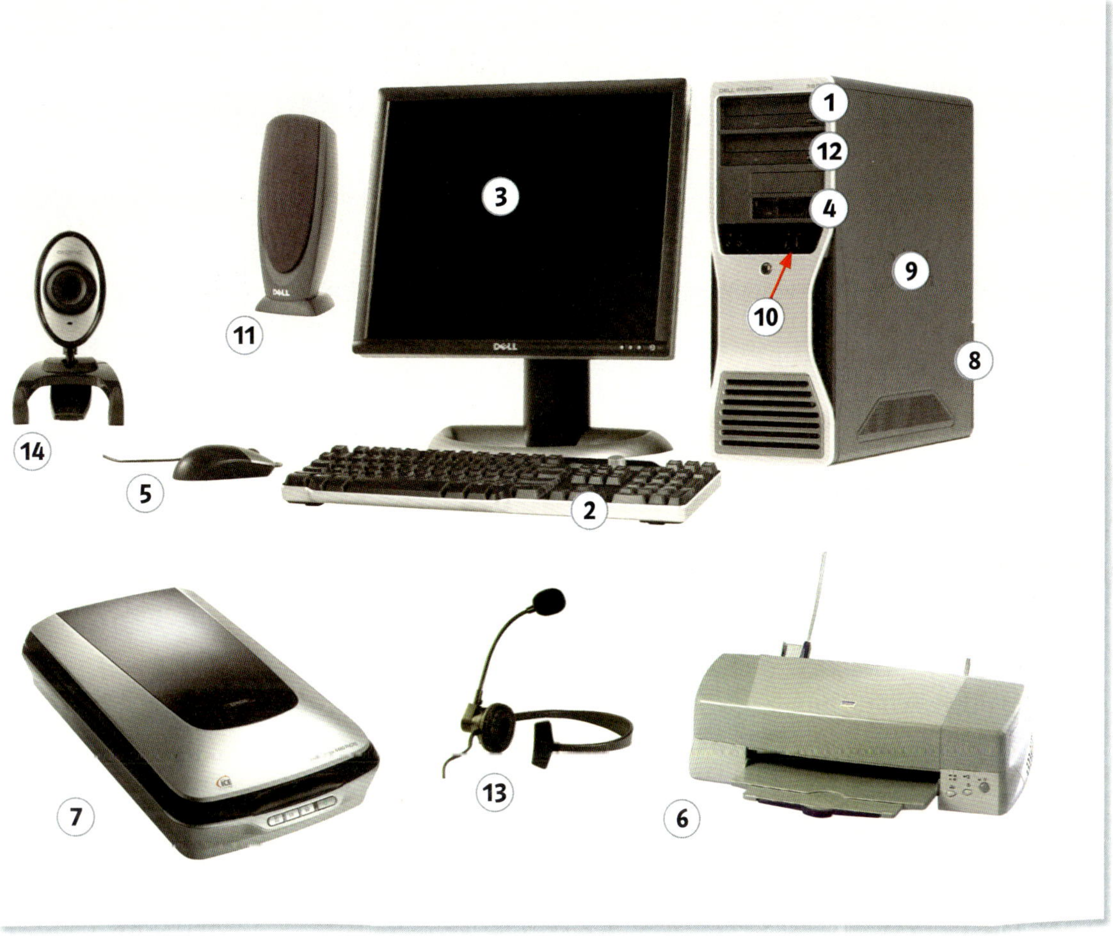

1. DVD drive
2. ______
3. ______
4. ______
5. ______
6. ______
7. ______
8. integrated modem
9. hard disk
10. ______
11. ______
12. ______
13. ______
14. ______

disk drive Diskettenlaufwerk	**integrated modem** integriertes Modem	**monitor** Bildschirm
DVD burner DVD Brenner		**mouse** Maus
DVD drive DVD-Laufwerk	**keyboard** Tastatur	**scanner** Bildabtaster, Scanner
hard disk Festplatte	**(laser) printer** (Laser-)Drucker	**USB port** USB-Port
headset Headset	**loudspeaker** Lautsprecher	**webcam** Webcam

1 Who is X?

In the late 1960s some mothers at his school in Seattle decided that it would be a good idea *to install* a computer and let the schoolchildren work and play on it.
He was thirteen years old then and he soon started to write his first *software program*. It was for playing *tic-tac-toe*. The first computer which he used was *huge* and slow. It did *not even* have a monitor. When the young people played they *typed in* their *moves* on a keyboard and then waited until the *results* came out of a noisy printer. A game of tic-tac-toe which usually takes thirty seconds with a pen and paper *lasted* half an hour then.
Later they started to *speed* things *up* on the computer and they made the games more difficult. One day a teacher who was teaching computer programming asked him for help and soon the boy was called the 'computer *guy*'.
As an adult he *realized* how exciting it had been that they could *control* such a heavy and *expensive* machine. They were too young to drive a car but they could give this machine *orders* and it *carried* them *out*.
Today this boy is the boss of the world's biggest software company and is one of the richest people in the world.

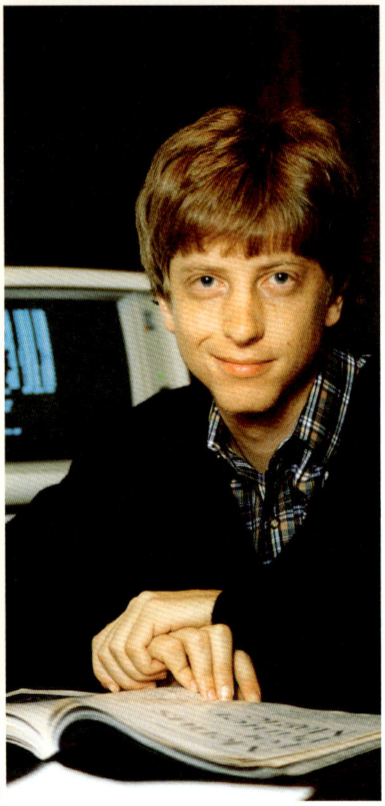

A Who is the text about?

Von wem handelt der Text?

His name is ______________________ .

B Compare the computer 30 years ago and the computer of today. Use the words in the box and information from the text.

Vergleichen Sie Computer von vor 30 Jahren und von heute.
Benutzen Sie die Wörter im Kasten und Informationen aus dem Text.

	30 years ago	today
speed ►		
noise ►		silent
price ►	expensive	
size ►		
weight ►		

heavy ~~expensive~~
small light big
cheap noisy
fast ~~silent~~ slow

in the late 1960s Ende der 60er Jahre
to install installieren, einsetzen
software program Computerprogramm
tic-tac-toe Spiel
huge riesig
not even noch nicht einmal
to type in eintippen
move (Spiel) Zug
result Ergebnis
to last dauern
to speed up schneller machen
guy Typ
as an adult als Erwachsener
he realized es wurde ihm klar
to control kontrollieren, beherrschen
order Befehl
to carry out ausführen
silent leise
size Größe

C **Work with a partner. Find the words which go together. Connect them to make pairs.**
Partnerarbeit. Welche Wortpaare passen zusammen? Verbinden Sie sie.

1. to write	**a)** an hour
2. to play	**b)** the results
3. to drive	**c)** tic-tac-toe
4. to last	**d)** a software program
5. to teach	**e)** a machine
6. *to print*	**f)** on the keyboard
7. to control	**g)** computer programming
8. to type something in	**h)** a car

D **Answer the questions on the text in 1.**
Beantworten Sie die Fragen über den Text in **1**.

1. What did some mothers install at Bill's school? Example: **They installed a computer.**
2. How old was Bill when he wrote his first program?
3. Where did he live when he was young?
4. What game did he like to play?
5. Who did he help later at school?
6. What is the boy's job today?

A game of tic-tac-toe

It's your turn now: X must move! Put a cross in the right box. Try to win in two moves.
Jetzt sind Sie dran! Setzen Sie ein Kreuz in das richtige Kästchen. Versuchen Sie in zwei Zügen zu gewinnen.

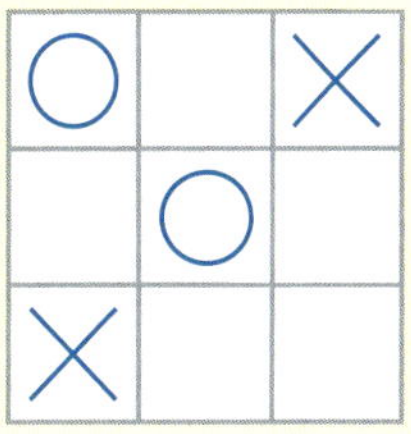

2 **A** **Write down short answers, depending on whether you have a computer or not.**
Schreiben Sie kurze Antworten, je nachdem, ob Sie einen Computer haben oder nicht.

1. Have you got a computer?

Yes ______________ No ______________

2. a) What do you use it for? ______________

2. b) Would you like to have one? ______________

3. a) How much time do you spend on it? ______________

3. b) If yes, what would you use it for? ______________

4. What will you need a computer for in the future? ______________

B **Now report to the class.**
Teilen Sie Ihre Antworten der Klasse mit.

to print drucken

3 There are a lot of customers in the computer shop.

Make one sentence from the two sentences which are given. Use who.
Verbinden Sie jeweils zwei Sätze mit **who**.

1. The girl wants to pay for the computer mouse. She is waiting at the *cash desk*.
   Example: **The girl who is waiting at the cash desk wants to pay for the computer mouse.**
2. The man wants to buy a scanner.
   He is talking to the *sales assistant*.
3. The young man wants to buy a new PC.
   He is looking at different types of computers.
4. The woman needs a printer.
   She has already bought a PC.
5. The boys are looking for new computer games.
   They are talking to each other.

4 A **Choose the correct ending for the sentences in 1–5. Connect them to make pairs.**
Suchen Sie das richtige Ende für jeden Satzanfang. Verbinden Sie sie.

1. This is the new customer service center	**a)** it is as big as a TV *screen*.
2. This is the new computer shop	**b)** it offers you help when you need it.
3. This is the new printer	**c)** it can show you a picture of the *caller*.
4. This is the new monitor	**d)** it sells everything for computer freaks.
5. This is the new telephone	**e)** it prints 30 pages per minute.

B **Write the sentences as relative clauses. Use which.**
Schreiben Sie die Sätze als Relativsätze auf. Benutzen Sie **which**.

Example: **This is the new customer service centre which offers you help when you need it.**

5 **Describe the people or things. Use the verbs in the blue box, the words below and the structure in the green box.**
Beschreiben Sie die Leute bzw. Dinge. Benutzen Sie die Verben im blauen Kasten, die unten stehenden Wörter und die Struktur im grünen Kasten.

A … is a	person thing machine	who … which …

run	know	buy
sell	wash	send

1. a shop manager
   Example: **A shop manager is a person who *runs a shop*.**
2. a washing machine
3. a customer
4. a computer freak
5. a sales assistant
6. a fax machine

cash desk	Kasse	**screen**	Bildschirm	**to run a shop**	ein Geschäft leiten
sales assistant	Verkäufer/in	**caller**	Anrufer/in		

6 A Complete the email. Fill in who or which.
Vervollständigen Sie das E-Mail mit **who** oder **which**.

Subject: New PC
From: Mark mark@cool.eu
To: lisa@cool.eu

Hi Lisa,

At last I've got the PC (1) ____________ I've always wanted to buy. I bought it on Saturday in the computer shop (2) ____________ is near the High Street. I *spent* all the money (3) ____________ I had saved. It's the fastest computer (4) ____________ I've ever seen. Now I can *contact* friends (5) ____________ live *all over the world* in seconds. A friend (6) ____________ moved to Newcastle some months ago has already sent me an email.

How are things? Have you still got the teacher (7) ____________ does computing on the *board*? My teacher is okay. She knows all the tricks (8) ____________ we want to know. That's all for now.

Hope to hear from you soon.

:-) Mark

B Do exercise 6A again. Leave out the relative pronoun where possible.
Machen Sie Übung **6A** noch einmal. Lassen Sie das Relativpronomen weg, wo es möglich ist.

to spend ausgeben
to contact Kontakt aufnehmen
all over the world auf der ganzen Welt
board Tafel

Relative clauses Relativsätze

Relativsätze werden verwendet, um eine Person oder Sache näher zu beschreiben. Sie werden mit einem Relativpronomen eingeleitet.

Anwendung

The girls who / that are taking part in the computer course are very interested.	Bei Personen werden die Relativpronomen who oder that verwendet.
This is the shop which / that is offering PCs at low prices.	Bei Sachen wird which oder that verwendet.
The shop assistant (who) I asked for help was very polite. The computer (which) I bought was cheap.	Wenn das Relativpronomen Objekt des Satzes ist, kann es weggelassen werden.

7 The computer has mixed up the following two texts for tomorrow's 'The Evening Post'.

Work with a partner. Underline the words which are in the wrong place. Then write the two stories again so that they make sense.
Partnerarbeit. Unterstreichen Sie die Wörter, die an der falschen Stelle stehen. Schreiben Sie dann die beiden Texte, so dass sie einen Sinn ergeben.

Living without the net?

The Evening Post

Dear Sir,
Why should I read a book or a school? Why should I know out? All I need is my PC and a modem to surf the *personnel managers*. Here she can *chat* all night with interesting people all over the world, can get all the information I need, and can *download* music or streets. So what else should I ask for? The only problem has that our training programme is now very high. I must talk to a job about that.
Yours,
Thomas Davies

Joanne Woodward (17) left newspaper a year ago. She didn't exactly go what she wanted to do. She had some interviews with the internet of some companies in her home town. But I wasn't really interested. She liked *hanging around* with friends in the videos. But soon she found that boring, too. So now she is *made up her mind* to start something new. She is taking part in a phone *bill* for young *unemployed* people. Here she can learn new *skills* which she will need in my parents. We hope she's on the right way now.

8 Today the students want to write letters to 'The Evening Post'. On the computer course the teacher is just giving instructions to the students on how to use the PC for writing letters.

A **Listen to the CD. Put the instructions in the right order.**
Hören Sie die CD. Bringen Sie die Anweisungen in die richtige Reihenfolge.

☐	*save* the text	☐	type your letter
☐	open a new *file*	☐	*load* the program
1	switch on the computer	☐	*switch off* the computer
☐	*close* the file	☐	leave the program
☐	print the text	☐	*format* the text

B **Write the instructions in complete sentences. Don't change the order. Begin the sentences with words from the box.**
Schreiben Sie die Anweisungen in ganzen Sätzen in der richtigen Reihenfolge auf. Fangen Sie die Sätze mit Wörtern aus dem Kasten an.

first | then | and then | finally | after that

Example: **First switch on the computer.**

Dear Sir (Leserbrief) Anrede	**to make up one's mind** sich entscheiden	**file** Datei
personnel manager Personalchef/in	**bill** Rechnung	**to close** schließen
to chat sich unterhalten	**unemployed** arbeitslos	**to load** laden
to download herunterladen	**skill** Fähigkeit, Fertigkeit	**to switch off** ausschalten
to hang around herumhängen	**to save** speichern	**to format** formatieren

The world of work

12

1. office worker

2. g

3. e

4. r

5. d a

6. l

A **Write the names of the jobs below the photos. Use the syllables in the box.**
Schreiben Sie die Berufsbezeichnungen unter die Fotos.
Benutzen Sie die Silben im Kasten.

as – cep – cian – den – doc – elec – ry
lor – ~~er~~ – er – er – ~~fice~~ – gar – ist – ~~of~~ – re
driv – sis – tant – tion – tor's – tri – ~~work~~

B **Choose four of the jobs above and say / write what these people normally do in their jobs.**
Wählen Sie vier der abgebildeten Jobs. Sagen / schreiben Sie, was die Leute normalerweise in ihren Jobs machen.

Example: **An office worker works at a computer.**

C **Choose any job. Don't tell anyone what it is. Make a typical movement that has to do with your job. Let the others guess what job it is. Answer only YES or NO.**
Wählen Sie irgendeinen Job. Sagen Sie ihn niemandem. Machen Sie eine job-typische Bewegung. Die anderen müssen den Job erraten. Antworten Sie nur mit JA oder NEIN.

Example: **Do you help people?** – Yes / No.

1

Modern Apprenticeships

- **Are you ready to learn new skills?**
- **Do you want to get top qualifications?**
- **Do you want to have a good job?**

Modern Apprenticeships are a real *chance* for you to get into the world of work. They offer real jobs with pay and training. At the same time you can study at college.

How old should I be?

Mainly it is for the 16- and 17-year-old *school leavers*, but if you are a little older you can also *apply*. You must finish your Modern Apprenticeship before your 25th birthday.

What qualifications can I get?

The new Apprenticeships give you the chance to train to NVQ* *Level* 3. At the same time you are *employed* and can earn money. *In addition* you learn skills such as *communication* or teamwork.

How long does it take?

Between two and a half and three and a half years.

What jobs can I train for?

You can work and train as a hairstylist, a car mechanic or a shop assistant, you can work in a bank or in a hospital, almost everything is possible.

* NVQ = National Vocational Qualification

Ross Hancock was glad when he was offered a Modern Apprenticeship with UK Paper in Sittingbourne, Kent. "It's *exactly* what I want," he says. "I'm getting training for a job, and money."

Ross spent his first year *full-time* at a training centre where he learnt practical skills in *engineering* and *paper-making*. He also went to college one day a week. Ross has now started with UK Paper for *on-the-job training* and is working *towards* an NVQ Level 3. "I'm happy to get as many qualifications as I can," says Ross.

apprenticeship Berufsausbildung, Lehre
chance Chance
mainly hauptsächlich
school leaver Schulabgänger/in
to apply sich bewerben
level Stufe
to be employed angestellt sein
in addition zusätzlich
communication Kommunikation
between zwischen
exactly genau
full-time Vollzeit
engineering Technik; Maschinenbau
paper-making Papierherstellung
on-the-job training innerbetriebliche Ausbildung
towards auf … zu

A **Answer the following questions. The correct numbers are in the text in 1.**
Beantworten Sie folgende Fragen. Die richtigen Zahlen finden Sie im Text in **1**.

1. How old are people who start a Modern Apprenticeship? They're ______________ to ______________ years old.
2. How long does a Modern Apprenticeship take? Between ______________ years and ______________ years.
3. What level of qualification can you get? Level ______________
4. How many years did Ross spend at a training centre? ______________ year(s)

B **List five things that a Modern Apprenticeship offers young people.**
Nennen Sie fünf Dinge, die eine moderne Berufsausbildung jungen Leuten bietet.

1. ______________
2. ______________
3. ______________
4. ______________
5. skills (communication and teamwork)

C **Find the words in the text in 1 and complete the puzzle.**
Suchen Sie die Wörter im Text in **1** und vervollständigen Sie das Rätsel.

1			Q		A										
2			P		P										
3			E		P										
4		L			R										
5				T	E										
6			B		N										
7		C			T										
8		T			I										
9	C				C										
10		M			E										
11					S	K	I	L	L	S					
12		M			H										
13				B	I										
14		H			P										

D **Make meaningful sentences with seven of the words from the puzzle.**
Schreiben Sie sinnvolle Sätze mit sieben der Wörter aus dem Rätsel.

Example: One of the skills I can learn is communication.

2 **A** **Sue and Terry are new *apprentices* with a big company. This is what happens at the beginning of their time there. First fill in the third form of the following verbs.**
Vervollständigen Sie die Tabelle mit der „3. Form" des Verbs.

1. train trained	**5.** give ______
2. teach taught	**6.** tell ______
3. *inform* ______	**7.** pay ______
4. show ______	**8.** take ______

B **Fill in the passive to talk about Sue and Terry. Choose one of the verbs in 2A.**
Vervollständigen Sie die Sätze mit der Passivform. Benutzen Sie eins der Verben in **2A**.

1. First they ______ the different *departments*.
2. Then Terry is taken to the *sales* department to start his training there.
3. They ______ help by their *trainers*.
4. Terry ______ £35 a week.
5. They ______ from 9.15 till 4.30.
6. One day a week they ______ at college.
7. They ______ that they must go to college on Thursday.
8. They are told to be at college at 9 o'clock in the morning.

3 **When Terry meets *some* of his new *colleagues* for the first time they ask him some questions. Fill in the suitable question tags from the box and the correct short answers.**
Vervollständigen Sie die Fragen der neuen Kollegen an Terry mit den passenden Frageanhängseln aus dem Kasten und den richtigen Kurzantworten.

1. You are Terry Cunningham, aren't you?
   Yes, I am.
2. You live in Moston, don't you?
   Yes, I do.
3. You don't have a younger brother, do you?
   No, I ______ .
4. You were at Manchester College, ______ ?
   Yes, ______ .

~~don't you?~~
can't you?
haven't you?
don't you?
weren't you?
~~aren't you?~~
~~do you?~~
doesn't she?
do you?

apprentice Auszubildende/r, Lehrling
to inform informieren
department Abteilung
sales Vertrieb
trainer Ausbilder/in
some einige
colleague Kollege, Kollegin

5. Your mother works in a supermarket, ____________________ ?
   Yes, ____________________ .
6. You can come to work by bike, ____________________ ?
   Yes, ____________________ .
7. You love football, ____________________ ?
   Yes, ____________________ .
8. You have watched a Manchester United *match*, ____________________ ?
   Yes, ____________________ .
9. You don't play football, ____________________ ?
   No, ____________________ .

4 **Here is some information about Sue, the other new apprentice.**
Ask her questions as in 3.
Stellen Sie Sue ähnliche Fragen wie in Übung 3.

Example: **You live with your father and mother, don't you?**

Sue Parker 18 years 29 High Street lives with her father and mother
no brothers or sisters left college last year loves dancing, doesn't play ball games

match Spiel

The passive Das Passiv

Terry **is paid** £35 a week. These cars **were made** in England.	Form von be in der jeweiligen Zeit + 3. Form Verbs
New workers **must be** trained first. The job **can be done**.	auch mit Hilfsverben + be + 3. Form

► **Anwendung**

He was introduced by the manager.	Hauptsächliche Verwendung in der Schriftsprache. Ist der Ausführende bekannt und seine Nennung wichtig, so wird er mit by angehängt.

Question tags Frageanhängsel

Aussagesatz	Frageanhängsel	
You are 25 years old,	**aren't you?**	Das Hilfsverb bzw. eine Form von be oder have wird in dem Frageanhängsel wiederholt.
You can work on Saturdays, You can't start now,	**can't you?** **can you?**	Ist der Aussagesatz bejaht, wird das Frageanhängsel verneint (und umgekehrt).
You worked in a hospital, She likes that work,	**didn't you?** **doesn't she?**	

5 A Three young people are talking about their courses at college. Listen to the CD. Fill in the missing information.
Hören Sie die CD. Schreiben Sie die fehlenden Informationen auf.

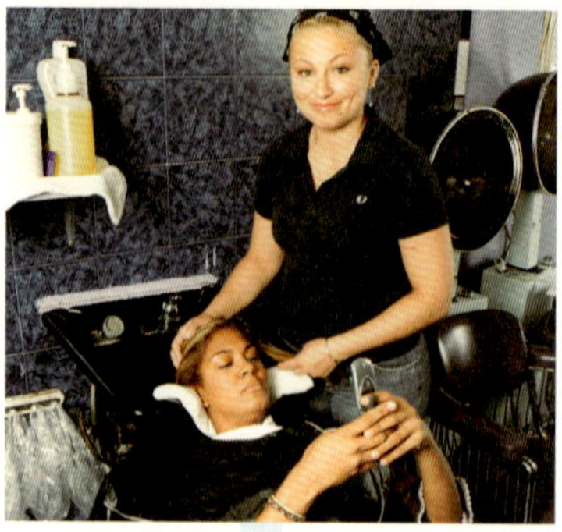

	1	2	3
name ►			
age ►			
job ►			

B Listen to the CD again and find out about the following.
Hören Sie die CD noch einmal. Schreiben Sie weitere Informationen auf.

	1	2	3
name of college ►			
year of training ►			
person who told them about the job ►			

C Write a few sentences about one of the three young people.
Schreiben Sie einige Sätze über eine der drei Personen.

6 Talk / write about yourself. Give your name, age, the name of your college, the job you would like to do and why, how you found out about that job etc.
Sprechen / Schreiben Sie über sich (Name, Alter, Name Ihrer Schule, welchen Job Sie gerne machen möchten und warum, wie Sie von diesem Beruf / Job erfahren haben usw.).

hairstylist	Frisörin	**carpenter**	Schreiner/in	**advice**	Rat(schlag)
experience	Erfahrung	**course guide**	Kursübersicht		

Tests

Test 1: One click away from prison

Test 2: Australia – only a dream?

Test 3: Cool or criminal?

Test 4: The happiest workers

Test 1 One click away from prison

Maybe Susan Sisley, 36, a shop assistant from Liverpool has to go to prison soon. Why?
She has done nothing wrong. The problem is that her 14-year-old son David loves music. He loves music so much that he has downloaded thousands of songs from the internet. She is responsible for her son and so she received a bill of three thousand pounds from the music industry for her son's downloads but she does not have the money. And that could put her in prison.
"I don't know anything about computers," Susan Sisley says. "I thought David needed his PC for school but now I've found out that he copied his favourite music most of the time. And I don't know where I can get the money from," she adds. "So maybe I have to go to prison instead."
David says that he really did not think about what he was doing. "Everyone I know at school does it. I didn't know it was wrong," he says.
Illegal downloads are a big problem for the music industry. "Sometimes you can download new CDs from the internet before you can buy them in the shops in Britain or in Germany," a manager of a big record company says. "And there's another trend today. Many people, especially teenagers, also download ring tones for their mobile phones. We have lost billions of pounds in that way and many musicians – most of them aren't stars, you know – need the money to live." (252 Wörter)

1 Questions on the text

Answer the following questions in English. Write complete sentences.

a) Where does Susan Sisley live?
b) Does she have any children?
c) What is David interested in?
d) What has David done?
e) How much does Susan have to pay?
f) What happens if she cannot pay the money?
g) Did Susan know that David copied songs from the internet?
h) What happens when a new CD comes out in America?
i) What is the latest trend with teenagers?
j) Why are illegal downloads a problem for the music industry?
k) Why should people pay for CDs or downloads?
l) Do you have a mobile phone? Give two reasons why or why not.

2 Vocabulary

2.1 What is the opposite of these words?
Example: nothing (line 5) ⟷ **everything**
a) to love (line 7) **b)** everyone (line 23) **c)** wrong (line 25)
d) before (line 29) **e)** to buy (line 29) **f)** big (line 31)

2.2 Give a synonym (= a word which has nearly the same meaning).
Example: PC (line 17) = **computer**
a) to receive (line 10) **b)** industry (line 11) **c)** teenagers (line 33)

2.3 Find the words in the text.
Example: billions = **many millions**
a) … = building in which young people learn **b)** … = person who sells things

Now you give the definition.
c) favourite (line 18) **d)** musicians (line 36)

2.4 Fill in the missing prepositions.
"I'm very interested (a) **in** music, so I often download songs (b) … the internet. (c) … school we often talk (d) … new CDs and our favourite stars. In the evening I often listen (e) … new songs with my friend. He usually comes (f) … seven and stays (g) … one or two hours."

2.5 A friend from England is staying with you. What would you say?
a) Sie wollen wissen, wie es ihm geht. Example: **How are you?**
b) Sie fragen ihn, welche Musik er mag.
c) Sie wollen wissen, ob er die neue CD von Sarah Williams gehört hat.
d) Sie sagen ihm, dass Sie ihre Musik sehr mögen.
e) Sie schlagen vor, diese CD zu hören.

2.6 Name three things that you can download from the internet.

3 Grammar

3.1 Give short answers.
Example: Do you like music? – **Yes, I do.**
a) Are you sixteen? Yes, …
b) Have you heard of Sarah Williams? No, …
c) Did you go to the show last night? Yes, …
d) Did you see my friend Tracy? No, …

3.2 Put the verbs in brackets into the past tense.
Susan (live) (a) **lived** in Liverpool and (work) (b) … as a shop assistant. She (not have) (c) … a lot of money. Her son David (go) (d) … to school. In the evening they (watch) (e) … TV together or David (play) (f)… on his PC. But one day Susan (get) (g) … a letter …

3.3 Fill in the comparatives and superlatives: '-er/est' or 'more/most'.
Example: Mobile phones are (expensive) **more expensive** than telephones at home.
a) Young people find them (exciting) … than normal phones.
b) Usually they are (small) … and (comfortable) … . You can even take photos!
c) But teenagers today are not (happy) … than young people twenty years ago who did not have mobile phones.

4 Translation

Translate the text into German.
In the last twenty years life has changed a lot. In nearly every home today there is a PC which connects us with billions of people by the internet. We can receive information from all over the world. We can also watch films on the computer, listen to English radio programmes, play PC games or telephone. At weekends young people have parties where they play computer games for twenty-four hours and sometimes even longer!

Test 2 Australia – only a dream?

When Christian was a little boy, he only had one dream. He wanted to go to Australia. So his parents bought him books about Australia and he put up posters of kangaroos and koala bears in his room. When he was sixteen, his dream came true. An exchange organization found a family and a place at an Australian high school for him.
It was very exciting for Christian because he had never made such a long journey alone. After twenty-four hours he arrived in Melbourne where his new family was waiting for him at the airport.
Christian's new parents were from Greece and had come to live in Australia twenty years ago. So Christian did not only learn about Australia but he also learned about the Greek way of life! The family had a lot of relatives and friends who often met and had barbecues. The food was quite different. They had a lot of fast food for dinner and so Christian put on weight during his stay. The weather was also a surprise to him. When he arrived in August, it was still winter in Australia!
High school was not too difficult because he could choose his courses. At the weekends the family took Christian on trips to interesting places near Melbourne or they went fishing. The year passed quickly and soon it was time to say goodbye.
Back in Germany Christian often thinks of his time in Melbourne and he is sure that he will go back to Australia one day!

(257 Wörter)

1 Questions on the text

Answer the following questions in English. Write complete sentences.

a) What did Christian dream of when he was young?
b) What did he get from his parents?
c) What animals did he like?
d) What did he do when he was sixteen?
e) How long did the journey to Australia take?
f) Why did Christian also learn a lot about the Greek way of life?
g) What food did he often eat in Australia?
h) What time of year is it in Australia in August?
i) What did he and his family do at the weekends?
j) How long did Christian stay in Australia?
k) What will Christian do one day?
l) Would you like to stay in another country for a year? Give two reasons why or why not.

2 Vocabulary

2.1 What is the opposite of these words?
Example: bought (line 4) ⟷ **sold**

a) never (line 12) **b)** long (line 12) **c)** arrive in (line 13) **d)** new (line 14)
e) winter (line 27) **f)** difficult (line 29) **g)** quickly (line 34) **h)** goodbye (line 35)

2.2 Give a synonym (= a word which has nearly the same meaning).
Example: arrive in (line 13) = **reach**

a) a lot of (line 21) **b)** pass (line 33) **c)** think of (line 36)

2.3 Find the words in the text.
Example: **parents** = father and mother

a) … = uncles, aunts, cousins **b)** … = country in the south of Europe

Now give the definitions.

e) family (line 9) **f)** Melbourne (line 14) **g)** airport (line 15)

2.4 Fill in the missing prepositions.

When Christian arrived (a) in Australia his new family was already there at the airport. As he was late they had to wait (b) … two hours there. Then they went home (c) … car. Christian was happy (d) … his new life in Australia. (e)… school he did not have any big problems. (f) … the end of his stay in Australia he knew a lot (g) … the fifth continent.

2.5 Complete the dialogue. What would you say?
A = Australian family, Y = you

a) A: Hallo, you must be Christian. How are you? – Y: Fine, thanks.
b) A: This is my husband Christos. – Y: …
c) A: Did you have a nice journey? – Y: …
d) A: Why was your plane late? – Y: …
e) A: You must be hungry. What would you like to eat? – Y: …
f) A: Let's drive home then. – Y: …

3 Grammar

3.1 Write down the plural form of the following nouns.

Example: boy – boys

a) journey **b)** book **c)** family **d)** life

3.2 Ask questions about the underlined parts of the sentences.

Example: Christian arrived in Melbourne. Where did he arrive?

a) His plane was late because the weather was bad.
b) In Australia Christian saw a lot of interesting places.
c) At the moment Christian is staying in London.
d) He will go to Australia again next year.

3.3 Fill in the correct forms: comparatives or superlatives (-er/-est, more/most or irregular forms).

Example: Australia is (big) bigger than Germany.

a) The weather is (good) … than in Germany.
b) Usually it is (warm) … in Australia.
c) It is (exciting) … to travel through Australia than Germany.
d) Christian thinks that kangaroos are the (interesting) … animals in the world.

3.4 Add question tags.

Example: You're from Germany, aren't you?

a) You've already eaten, …?
b) Your parents live in Stuttgart, …?
c) You don't have a sister, …?
d) Your friend David isn't in Australia, …?

4 Translation

Translate the text into German.

Many German teenagers go to America for a year. They usually stay in families there and go to an American high school. Most people say that this is the best way to learn the language. And of course, you also get to know the country.

At first it is difficult for young people to leave their families in Germany. But after a time they make new friends and enjoy life in their new homes. So, when they have to leave America after a year, they often feel unhappy.

Test 3 Cool or criminal?

A shopping centre has forbidden hooded tops or "hoodies". Young people who wear hooded tops are not allowed to enter this shopping centre any more. The managers of the shopping centre see this type of clothing as a symbol of crime and violence. For the shopping centre the ban will make the shopping centre safer for families.

Also at a school in the same town, they have forbidden hoodies. The teachers in the school want to stop pupils hiding their faces. This often happens when pupils are breaking rules. But many young people wear this type of clothing not because they want to be criminal or anti-social. They really want to be fashionable and cool. Many experts on young people do not think that the bans are good. They say that young people must have the right to wear what they like. Also they think that most of the young people who wear hoodies work hard at school. The young people have fun and do not get into trouble. They grow up into hard-working adults. The experts say that schools and shopping centres have to look at the problems. But at the same time they must not think that all teenagers who wear these types of clothes are criminals. (212 Wörter)

1 Questions on the text

Answer the following questions in English. Write complete sentences.

a) What has a shopping centre done?
b) How do the managers there see hoodies?
c) How will the ban on hoodies help?
d) What other place has forbidden hoodies?
e) What do the teachers want?
f) Why do teenagers wear hoodies?
g) Who does not want the bans on hoodies?
h) Why do they think the bans are not good?
i) How are most of the teenagers who wear hoodies?
j) What do the experts say?
k) What must schools and shopping centres not do?
l) What do you think? Must schools forbid hoodies?

2 Vocabulary and language

2.1 What is the opposite of these words?

Example: good (line 21) ⟷ **bad**

a) forbid (line 2) **b)** safe (line 9) **c)** same (line 11)
d) breaking (line 15) **e)** adults (line 27)

2.2 Give a synonym (= a word which has nearly the same meaning).

Example: hooded top = **hoodie**

a) young people (line 3) **b)** enter (line 4) **c)** clothing (line 7)
d) type (line 7) **e)** hard (line 25)

2.3 Find the words in the text.

Example: **hoodies** = sweatshirts which are hooded

a) … = a place with many shops
b) … = a person who does a crime

Now you give the definition.

c) pupil

2.4 Name 6 types of clothing.

2.5 Complete the dialogue.
A young person wants to go shopping in a shopping centre.
He / she is stopped by a manager there. What do they say?

a) Manager: Sagen Sie, dass er nicht hereinkommen kann.
Example: **You are not allowed to enter.**
b) Manager: Sagen Sie, dass es verboten ist, hoodies zu tragen.
c) Young person: Fragen Sie, warum Sie keine hoodies tragen dürfen.
d) Manager: Erklären Sie, dass Sie das Zentrum für alle sicherer machen wollen.
e) Young person: Erklären Sie, dass nicht alle, die hoodies tragen, kriminell sind.
f) Manager: Sagen Sie, dass es Ihnen leid tut, aber es gibt eine neue Regel.
g) Young person: Sagen Sie, dass Sie das Recht haben, das zu tragen, was Sie wollen.

3 Grammar

3.1 Put the verbs in brackets into the correct tense.
It is difficult for young people to talk about their problems. The problems often (depend) (a) **depend** on where they live and who their family and friends (be) (b) … . Last year some young people (start) (c) … a project called "Make Space". This gives young people a chance to say what they want. "Make Space" (meet) (d) … in June last year to discuss problems such as crime and violence. Next year they (organize) (e) … more projects. They (meet) (f) … again in Leeds and London next year.

3.2 Ask for the underlined part of the sentence.
a) Last week a school in Britain banned hoodies.
b) Managers have forbidden them in a shopping centre, too.
c) Experts on young people said that the ban was not correct.
d) Most young people work hard at school.

3.3 Add question tags.
Example: Tom likes to wear hoodies, **doesn't he?**
a) Many experts think this ban is unfair, … ?
b) The managers don't understand us, … ?
c) Some people have heard about the ban, … ?

3.4 Give short answers to these questions.
Example: Do you like to go to the shopping centre? **Yes, I do.**
a) Does Sam wear hoodies? Yes, …
b) Have you heard about the ban? Yes, …
c) Has Jenny been in school this week? No, …
d) Did you see the programme on crime in shopping centres last night? No, …

4 Translation

Translate the text into German.
Camila Turner, a student at Newcastle College says this in an interview: "Good schools with rules are important for young people. But home life is just as important. Parents must be more responsible for their children and make better homes for them. Some children grow up in a home where crime and violence are seen as normal. What these children need is not cool sports centres and computer courses. They need good friends who they can meet and who they can talk to."

Test 4 The happiest workers

Who do you think is happiest in their job? Is it a hairdresser, a plumber or an architect? The answer is surprising. A survey of 1,249 workers in Britain found that hairdressers were the happiest. Plumbers were in fifth place and architects were last in the list of 29 jobs. So what makes hairdressers so happy at work? Hairdressing is great if you get on well with people and like doing creative work. Interviews with hairdressers show that many of them love their job. John Skinner, a hairdresser from Nottingham, told the newspaper journalist: "Hairdressing is a good job and it helps you to stay young. You meet a lot of different people so it isn't boring." Another hairdresser, Penny Smith from Glasgow, said: "You are like a psychologist because you have to listen to people's problems. At the same time you are making them look good. Then they begin to feel better and they see themselves in a more positive light." The work has some disadvantages, too. The pay is only good when you get to the top. Also, there can be health risks when you stand the whole day. You can also get allergic reactions from the chemicals you use. The working day is long and you have to work on Saturdays. Most customers like the way the hairdresser does their hair, but some people are unfriendly and difficult to please. (236 Wörter)

1 Questions on the text

Answer the following questions in English. Write complete sentences.

a) How many people did the survey?
b) Which group of people were the happiest in their jobs?
c) Which group of people were the unhappiest?
d) When is hairdressing a great job?
e) Why is hairdressing not boring?
f) Why is a hairdresser like a psychologist?
g) How do hairdressers help people?
h) How is the pay in hairdressing?
i) Which health problems can hairdressers have?
j) What other disadvantages are there of hairdressing?
k) How do the customers react?
l) What would you like to become? Why?

2 Vocabulary and language

2.1 What is the opposite of these words?

Example: happiest (line 1) ⟷ **saddest**

a) boring (line 18) **b)** better (line 24)
c) long (line 31) **d)** difficult (line 35)

2.2 Find the words in the text.

Example: **plumber** = a person who fixes broken water pipes

a) … = a meeting with a person to ask them questions
b) … = a person who writes for a newspaper
c) … = the money you get for your work
d) … = a medical problem when you react to something

Now you give the definitions.

Example: architect = **a person who designs houses**

e) hairdresser
f) disadvantage

2.3 Write down the nouns from these words.
Example: think ⟶ **thought**
a) surprising **b)** happy **c)** different **d)** feel

3 Grammar

3.1 Ask for the underlined parts of the sentence.
Example: Penny Smith comes from Glasgow. – **Where does Penny Smith come from?**
a) She told us what she likes about her job.
b) I like my job because it's creative.
c) They carried out the survey in 2005.

3.2 Put the verbs in brackets into the right tense.
In Britain you (not / need) (a) **don't need** special qualifications to work in a hairdresser's salon. A good salon (train) (b) … beginners and (send) (c) … them to college. Last week we (speak) (d) … to Sam Law, a salon owner in Manchester. He (say) (e) …: "Training usually (take) (f) … 2 or 3 years. If you (become) (g) … a top stylist, you (be able to) (h) … earn £30,000 or more a year."

3.3 Fill in the comparatives and the superlatives.
Example: Hairdressers were the (happy) **happiest** of all the people in the survey.
a) Hairdressers were (high) … in the list than architects.
b) An architect gets (good) … pay than a hairdresser.
c) Working with people is (interesting) … than working alone.
d) Some customers are (difficult) … to please than others.

3.4 You are a hairdresser. What would you say to this customer?
a) You: …
Customer: Good morning
b) You: …
C: I'm fine, thanks.
c) You: …
C: Well. I'd like my hair to be shorter.
d) You: …
C: About 5 centimetres long.
(Zwanzig Minuten später.)
e) You: …
C: That's fine. Thank you.
f) You: …
C: Here you are. £15. Please keep the change.
g) You: …

4 Translation

Translate the text into German.
Training to become a plumber
A trained plumber does not usually have any difficulty in finding a job in Britain. There are not enough plumbers in Britain at the moment. The job can be very interesting. You meet a lot of people, colleagues as well as customers, and the work can be very creative. While plumbers do not earn much money during their training, the pay is good after they get their qualifications. After two years, a British plumber earns about £28,000 a year. A good plumber, who has his own company, can earn up to £40,000 a year.

Grundwortschatz

Diese Liste umfasst die Vokabeln, die für das Lehr- / Arbeitsbuch vorausgesetzt werden. Da nicht in allen Fällen Mehrfachbedeutungen in der Übersetzung angegeben werden können, ersetzt diese Liste nicht ein umfassendes zweisprachiges Wörterbuch.
Beim Verwenden der Liste als Übersetzungshilfe muss immer der Kontext beachtet werden.
Zahlwörter *(one, two, first, second ...)*, Pronomen *(I, you, my, your, myself, yourself ...)*, die Wochentage *(Monday, Tuesday ...)* sowie die Monatsnamen *(January, February ...)* sind nicht enthalten.

* = unregelmäßige Verbform

A

a, an ein/e
a little ein wenig
a lot viel/e
about über, um
across (quer) über (hinüber)
address Adresse
after nach, nachdem
afternoon Nachmittag
again wieder
air Luft
airport Flughafen
all alle/s
all right in Ordnung
always immer
a.m. vormittags
and und
animal Tier
answer antworten; Antwort
any irgendein/e/er
apple Apfel
around um (herum)
ask fragen
at an, in, zu
away weg

B

baby Baby
back zurück
bad schlecht
bag Tasche
ball Ball
banana Banane
bank Bank
baseball Baseball
bath Bad
bathroom Badezimmer
be* sein
beautiful schön
because weil
bed Bett
bedroom Schlafzimmer
before vor, bevor
begin* anfangen, beginnen
beginning Anfang, Beginn
big groß
bike Fahrrad
bird Vogel
birthday Geburtstag
black schwarz
blue blau
boat Boot
body Körper
book Buch
bottle Flasche
box Karton, Schachtel
boy Junge
bread Brot
break* (zer)brechen, kaputt machen
breakfast Frühstück
bring* bringen
brother Bruder
brown braun
building Gebäude
bus Bus
business Geschäft, Business
but aber
buy* kaufen
by durch, mit

C

cake Kuchen
call rufen, nennen, heißen; Anruf
camping Camping
can können
cannot (can't) nicht können
car Auto
careful vorsichtig
carry tragen
cat Katze
catch* fangen
centre Zentrum, Mitte
centimetre Zentimeter
chair Stuhl
cheap billig
check prüfen
cheese Käse
chicken Hähnchen
child Kind
chocolate Schokolade
Christmas Weihnachten
cigarette Zigarette
city Stadt
class Klasse
classroom Klassenzimmer
clean sauber; putzen
clever schlau, clever
clock Uhr
closed geschlossen
club Club
coach Reisebus; Trainer/in
coffee Kaffee
cold kalt
colour Farbe
come* kommen
computer Computer

cook kochen; Koch, Köchin
correct richtig; korrigieren
cost* kosten
could könnte/n, konnte/n
country Land
of course (not) natürlich (nicht)
cup Tasse
cut* schneiden; Schnitt

D

dad Papa
dance tanzen; Tanz
date Datum
daughter Tochter
day Tag
dead tot
dear lieb
deep tief
desk Schreibtisch
dictate diktieren
dictation Diktat
dinner Abendessen
discussion Diskussion
do* tun, machen
doctor Arzt, Ärztin
dog Hund
door Tür
down (nach) unten
dream* träumen; Traum
dress Kleid
drink* trinken; Getränk
drive* fahren
driver Fahrer/in
dry trocken

E

early früh
east (nach) Osten; östlich
easy leicht
eat* essen
empty leer; leeren
end beenden; Ende
England England
English englisch
evening Abend
every jede/r/s
exact genau
exam Prüfung
example Beispiel
exercise Übung
explain erklären
eye Auge

F

face Gesicht
fall* fallen; Sturz
false falsch
family Familie
fat dick; fett
father Vater
feel* fühlen
fill füllen
find* finden
film Film
fine gut, schön
finger Finger
finish aufhören, beenden
first erste/r/s; zuerst
fish fischen; Fisch
flower Blume
food Essen, Lebensmittel
foot Fuß
football Fußball
for für
forget* vergessen
form formen; Form
free frei; kostenlos
friend Freund/in
from von
fruit Frucht
full (of) voll (von, mit)

G

game Spiel
garage Garage
garden Garten
get* erhalten, bekommen, werden
get up aufstehen
girl Mädchen
give* geben
glass Glas
go* gehen, fahren
gold Gold
good gut
Goodbye. Auf Wiedersehen!
grandfather Großvater
grandmother Großmutter
grass Gras
great groß; großartig
green grün
group Gruppe

H

hair Haar
half halb
happy glücklich
have* (got) haben
head Kopf
hear* hören
heavy schwer
hello hallo
help helfen; Hilfe
here hier
high hoch
hobby Hobby
holiday(s) Ferien, Urlaub
home nach / zu Hause; Zuhause
homework Hausaufgaben
hope hoffen; Hoffnung
hospital Krankenhaus
hot heiß
hotel Hotel
hour Stunde
house Haus
how wie
how much wie viel
how old wie alt
hungry hungrig

I

ice cream Eis
idea Idee
if wenn, falls, ob
ill krank
in in
interest Interesse
interesting interessant
into in (hinein)

J

jacket Jacke
jeans Jeans
job Job

K

keep* (be)halten
kilo(gramme) Kilo(gramm)
kilometre Kilometer
king König
kiss küssen; Kuss
kitchen Küche
know* wissen

L

lady Dame
late spät
learn* lernen
left links; übrig
lesson Stunde
letter Brief
lie* (down) (sich hin)legen; liegen
life Leben
light hell; leicht; Licht
like mögen; wie
line Linie
list Liste
listen (to) zuhören
litre Liter
little klein; wenig
live leben, wohnen
living room Wohnzimmer
long lang
look schauen, (aus)sehen; Blick
love lieben; Liebe
lucky Glück haben
lunch Mittagessen

M

machine Maschine
make* machen
man Mann, Mensch
many viele
marmalade Marmelade
metal Metall
metre Meter
middle Mitte
milk Milch
minute Minute
mistake Fehler
moment Moment
money Geld
month Monat
more mehr
morning Morgen
most meiste/r/s
mother Mutter
much viel
mum Mutter
music Musik
must müssen

N

name Name
need brauchen
never nie(mals)
new neu
news Nachricht(en)
newspaper Zeitung
next nächste/r/s
nice schön, nett, gut
night Nacht
no nein; kein
not nicht
nothing nichts
now jetzt
number Zahl, Nummer

O

o' clock (Uhr)
of von, bei, aus
off weg
office Büro
often oft
old alt
one ein/e
only nur
open öffnen; geöffnet
or oder
order bestellen; Bestellung
order befehlen
other andere/r/s
out aus
over über

P

page Seite
pair Paar
paper Papier
parents Eltern
park parken; Park
parking Parken
partner Partner/in
party Party
passenger Passagier/in
pay* (be)zahlen; Lohn
pen Füller; Stift
people Leute
person Person
phone anrufen; Telefon
photo Foto
picture Bild
place Ort
plan planen; Plan
plastic (aus) Plastik
play spielen; Theaterstück
player Spieler/in
p.m. nachmittags
police Polizei
policeman Polizist
poor arm
pop Pop
post office Post
postcard Postkarte
postman Postbote
press drücken; Presse
pretty hübsch
price Preis
programme Programm
pronounce aussprechen
pull ziehen
pupil Schüler/in
push schieben
put* stellen, legen, setzen
put on anziehen; auftragen

Q

queen Königin
question Frage
quick schnell

R

radio Radio
rain regnen; Regen
rainy regnerisch
read* lesen
record aufnehmen; Schallplatte
red rot
remember sich erinnern
repair reparieren
report berichten; Bericht
rest Rest
restaurant Restaurant
rich reich
ride* reiten
right rechts; richtig
ring* klingeln; Ring
river Fluss
road Straße
room Zimmer; Platz
round rund; um (herum)
run* laufen, rennen

S

sad traurig
safe sicher
same gleiche/r/s
sand Sand
sandwich Sandwich
say* sagen
school Schule

sea Meer
second zweite/r/s; Sekunde
see* sehen
sell* verkaufen
send* schicken, senden
sentence Satz
ship Schiff
shirt Hemd
shoe Schuh
shop Laden, Geschäft
short kurz
show* zeigen; Show
side Seite
sing* singen
single einzel/n
sister Schwester
sit* sitzen
sleep* schlafen; Schlaf
slow langsam
small klein
smoke rauchen; Rauch
so so
sock Socke
soft weich
some etwas, einige
son Sohn
song Lied, Song
(I'm) sorry! Entschuldigung!
soup Suppe
speak* sprechen
sport Sport
stand* stehen
start anfangen; Anfang
station Bahnhof
stop aufhören, anhalten; Halt
story Geschichte
street Straße
strong stark
stupid dumm
summer Sommer
sun Sonne
supermarket Supermarkt
swim* schwimmen

T

table Tisch
take* nehmen, mitnehmen
talk reden, sprechen
taxi Taxi
tea Tee
teach* unterrichten
teacher Lehrer/in
team Team
telephone telefonieren; Telefon
television Fernseher
tell* erzählen
text Text
thank (sich) bedanken
that (one) der / die / das da
the der / die / das
theatre Theater
then dann
there da, dort
these diese
thing Ding
think* denken, meinen
this diese/r/s
those jene
ticket (Fahr-/Eintritts)karte
time Zeit
today heute
together zusammen
toilet Toilette
tomato Tomate
tomorrow morgen
too auch; zu
top Spitze
tourist Tourist/in
town Stadt
train trainieren; Zug
translate übersetzen
tree Baum
trip Reise
trouble Ärger
true richtig; wahr
TV Fernseher

U

uncle Onkel
under unter
understand verstehen
until bis
us uns

V

very sehr
visit besuchen; Besuch

W

wake* up aufwachen
walk laufen, gehen
want wollen
warm warm
wash waschen
watch beobachten, anschauen
water Wasser
way Weg
week Woche
weekend Wochenende
well gut; gesund; also
what was
what about was ist mit
when wann
where wo(hin)
which welche/r/s
white weiß
who wer
whole ganz
why warum
will ('ll) werden
win gewinnen
winter Winter
with mit
woman Frau
word Wort
work arbeiten; Arbeit
write* schreiben
write down aufschreiben
wrong falsch

Y

year Jahr
yes ja
yesterday gestern
young jung

Z

zoo Zoo

Kapitelbegleitende Wortlisten

Die Übersetzungen beziehen sich auf den jeweiligen Kontext in der angegebenen Unit / Übung.

Abkürzungen und Symbole

AP Activity page
BE britisches Englisch
HV Hörverständnisübung
US amerikanisches Englisch
pl Plural (Mehrzahl)
S Starter- bzw. Auftakt-Seite

Phonetic alphabet Lautschrift

[ː] bedeutet, dass der vorangegangene Laut lang ist
[ˈ] bedeutet, dass die folgende Silbe eine Hauptbetonung erhält
[ˌ] bedeutet, dass die folgende Silbe eine Nebenbetonung erhält
[‿] bedeutet, dass die beiden Laute miteinander verbunden werden

[iː] meet [miːt]
[ɑː] father [ˈfɑːðə]
[ɔː] morning [ˈmɔːnɪŋ]
[uː] blue [bluː]
[ɜː] German [ˈdʒɜːmən]

[ɪ] in [ɪn]
[e] yes [jes]
[æ] thanks [θæŋks]
[ʌ] much [mʌtʃ]
[ɒ] what [wɒt]
[ʊ] good [gʊd]
[ə] number [ˈnʌmbə]

[eɪ] name [neɪm]
[aɪ] my [maɪ]
[ɔɪ] boiled [bɔɪld]
[əʊ] phone [fəʊn]
[aʊ] now [naʊ]
[ɪə] hear [hɪə]
[eə] where [weə]
[ʊə] tourist [ˈtʊərɪst]

[p] pop [pɒp]
[b] bye [baɪ]
[t] town [taʊn]
[d] drink [drɪŋk]
[k] coffee [ˈkɒfɪ]
[g] good [gʊd]
[tʃ] church [tʃɜːtʃ]
[dʒ] job [dʒɒb]
[f] fine [faɪn]
[v] very [ˈverɪ]
[θ] thanks [θæŋks]
[ð] this [ðɪs]

[s] son [sʌn]
[z] is [ɪz]
[ʃ] she [ʃiː]
[ʒ] television [ˌtelɪˈvɪʒn]
[h] he [hiː]
[m] my [maɪ]
[n] now [naʊ]
[ŋ] evening [ˈiːvnɪŋ]
[l] like [ˈlaɪk]
[r] room [ruːm]
[w] we [wiː]
[y] yes [yes]

Unit 1

1	**far** [fɑ:]	weit (weg / entfernt)	⟷ near
	farmer ['fɑ:mə]	Bauer, Farmer	farm ⟶ farmer
	flat [flæt]	Wohnung	There are three flats in the house.
	friendly ['frendlɪ]	nett, freundlich	friend ⟶ friendly
	grandparents ['græn,peərnts]	Großeltern	the mother and father of your parents
	housewife ['haʊswaɪf]	Hausfrau	A housewife works at home.
	Ireland ['aɪələnd]	Irland	Dublin is a city in Ireland.
	Italy ['ɪtəlɪ]	Italien	Rome is a city in Italy.
	kids [kɪdz]	Kinder / junge Leute	= children
	lots of ['lɒts əv]	viel(e)	I've got lots of CDs.
	mechanic [mɪ'kænɪk]	Mechaniker	A car mechanic works on cars.
	near [nɪə]	in der Nähe von	⟷ far
	next door [,nekst‿'dɔ:]	nebenan	The Wilsons live next door to us.
	older ['əʊldə]	älter	⟷ younger
	out of work [,aʊt‿əv 'wɜ:k]	arbeitslos	She's out of work and she can't find a job.
	really ['rɪəlɪ]	wirklich	The new film with Tom Cruise is really great.
	shop assistant ['ʃop‿ə,sɪstnt]	Verkäufer/in	a person who works in a shop
	ten years ago [,ten 'jɪəz ə,gəʊ]	vor 10 Jahren	We lived in Italy ten years ago.
1D	**family tree** [,fæməlɪ 'tri:]	Familien-Stammbaum	You can draw a family tree.
	field [fi:ld]	Feld	You play baseball on a field.
	member ['membə]	Mitglied	a person who is in a team
2	**brother-in-law** ['brʌðerɪnlɔ:]	Schwager	My sister lives in Dublin with my brother-in-law.
	cousin ['kʌzn]	Cousin, Cousine	David is Jenny's cousin and Jenny is David's cousin.
	great grandfather [,greɪt'grænd,fɑ:ðə]	Urgroßvater	your mother's or father's grandfather
	great grandmother [,greɪt'græn,mʌðə]	Urgroßmutter	your mother's or father's grandmother
	nephew ['nefju:]	Neffe	your brother's or sister's son
	niece [ni:s]	Nichte	your brother's or sister's daughter
	sister-in-law ['sɪstərɪnlɔ:]	Schwägerin	Your sister-in-law is not your sister.
3	**balcony** ['bælkənɪ]	Balkon	We sit on the balcony in summer.
4A	**armchair** ['ɑ:mtʃeə]	Sessel	a big chair in the living room
	carpet ['kɑ:pɪt]	Teppich	There is a blue carpet in the bedroom.
	chest of drawers [,tʃest əv 'drɔ:z]	Kommode	You put clothes into a chest of drawers.
	coffee table ['kɒfɪ ,teɪbl]	Couchtisch	a small table
	cooker ['kʊkə]	Herd	You cook food on an electric cooker or on a gas cooker.
	cupboard ['kʌbəd]	Schrank	You put cups into the cupboard.
	curtain ['kɜ:tn]	Vorhang	You close the curtains at night.
	downstairs [,daʊn'steəz]	unten (im Haus)	⟷ upstairs
	fridge [frɪdʒ]	Kühlschrank	You keep food cold in a fridge.
	lamp [læmp]	(Steh-)Lampe	A lamp gives us light.
	upstairs [ʌp'steəz]	oben (im Haus)	⟷ downstairs
	wardrobe ['wɔ:drəʊb]	Kleiderschrank	a cupboard for clothes
	window ['wɪndəʊ]	Fenster	Can we open the window?
4B	**shelf, shelves** [ʃelf, ʃelvz]	Regal, Regale	You keep books on a shelf.
4C	**storey** ['stɔ:rɪ]	Etage	The house has got three storeys.
	washbasin ['wɒʃ,beɪsn]	Waschbecken	You wash your hands in a washbasin.
5B	**hall** [hɔ:l]	Flur	a very big room
6HV	to **stretch out** [stretʃ 'aʊt]	sich ausgestreckt hinlegen	He stretched out on the sofa and went to sleep.

Symbole: ⟷ opposite ⟶ word family = synonym

Unit 1

8A	**argument** [ˈɑːgjəmənt]	Streit	I don't like arguments with my parents.
	endless [ˈendless]	endlos	the end ⟶ to end ⟶ endless
	not the way [ˌnɒt‿ðə ˈweɪ]	nicht so (wie)	The meal is not the way I want it to be.
	thin [θɪn]	dünn	If you don't eat, you'll get too thin.

Unit 2

S	**American** [əˈmerɪkən]	Amerikaner/in	Tom Hanks is an American.
	net [net]	Netz	tennis net
	small ad [ˌsmɔːl ˈæd]	Kleinanzeige	= advertisement
1	**a bit** [ə ˈbɪt]	ein bisschen	= a little
	atmosphere [ˈætməsfɪə]	Stimmung	The atmosphere at the party was great.
	brilliant [ˈbrɪlɪənt]	brillant, toll, genial	= great
	cinema [ˈsɪnəmə]	Kino	You watch films at the cinema.
	difficult [ˈdɪfɪklt]	schwierig	⟷ easy; a difficult test = a hard test
	to **draw** [drɔː]	zeichnen	We can draw a picture with our pens.
	drawing [ˈdrɔːɪŋ]	Zeichnung	a picture made with a pen
	during [ˈdjʊərɪŋ]	während	We mustn't eat during lessons at school.
	to **enjoy** [ɪnˈdʒɔɪ]	Spaß haben	The concert was great. I enjoyed it.
	gardener [ˈgɑːdnə]	Gärtner	a person who works in a garden
	gardening [ˈgɑːdnɪŋ]	Gartenarbeit	working in a garden
	hard [hɑːd]	schwierig	⟷ easy; a hard test = a difficult test
	to **hit** [hɪt]	schlagen	David's bike hit a stone.
	magazine [ˌmægəˈziːn]	Zeitschrift	Robert likes football magazines.
	neighbour [ˈneɪbə]	Nachbar	Your neighbour's house is next to your house.
	outdoors [ˌaʊtˈdɔːz]	draußen	= outside
	outside [ˌaʊtˈsaɪd]	draußen	⟷ inside; = outdoors
	reporter [rɪˈpɔːtə]	Reporter/in	= a journalist. A reporter works for a newspaper.
	rule [ruːl]	Regel	Can you find a rule for the plural forms?
	sometimes [ˈsʌmtaɪmz]	manchmal	never – sometimes – often – always
	to **spend** [spend]	verbringen	‚To spend' heißt nicht ‚spenden'.
	village [ˈvɪlɪdʒ]	Dorf	a village – a town – a city
3	to **send a text message** [ˌsend ə ˈtekst‿ˌmesɪdʒ]	eine SMS verschicken	She sends text messages to her friends.
4A	**boot** [buːt]	Stiefel	You wear boots in winter.
	to **choose** [tʃuːz; tʃəʊz]	aussuchen	Which colour pen do you want? You can choose.
	dark [dɑːk]	dunkel	You can't see when it's dark.
	to **fix a time** [ˌfɪks ə ˈtaɪm]	eine Zeit ausmachen	Can we fix a time to go to the cinema?
	large [lɑːdʒ]	groß	= big
	to **leave** [liːv]	verlassen	The train leaves at 6.54 a.m.
	to **meet** [miːt]	(sich) treffen (mit)	We can meet for lunch.
	to **sit down** [sɪt ˈdaʊn]	sich hinsetzen	⟷ to stand up
	to **stay alone** [steɪ‿əˈləʊn]	allein bleiben	She is fifteen. She can stay at home alone.
	usually [ˈjuːʒəlɪ]	normalerweise	Today Mark is playing golf. He usually plays football.
	what's on [ˌwɒts ˈɒn]	was läuft	What's on in the cinema?
	whistle [ˈwɪsl]	Pfeife; Anpfiff	When you hear the whistle, the game is finished.
5A	**cooking** [ˈkʊkɪŋ]	Kochen	I like cooking.
	dancing [ˈdɑːntsɪŋ]	Tanzen	I go dancing in the disco every Saturday.
	important [ɪmˈpɔːtnt]	wichtig	You must listen to the information. It's important!
	mate [meɪt]	Kumpel, Freund/in	= friend

Symbole: ⟷ opposite ⟶ word family = synonym

Unit 2

6A	**children's nurse** [ˌtʃɪldrənz 'nɜ:s]	Kinderkranken-schwester	A children's nurse looks after children in hospital.
	wish [wɪʃ]	Wunsch	Best wishes
6 HV	**exciting** [ɪk'saɪtɪŋ]	spannend, aufregend	⟷ boring
6B	**bungee jumping** ['bʌndʒɪ ˌdʒʌmpɪŋ]	Bungeejumping	Our teacher does bungee jumping.
	cybercafe ['saɪbəˌkæfeɪ]	Internet-Café	You can write emails to friends in a cybercafé.
	guitar [gɪ'tɑ:]	Gitarre	I can play the guitar well.
	unpaid [ʌn'paɪd]	unbezahlt	You don't get any money for unpaid work.

Unit 3

SA	**fashion** ['fæʃn]	Mode	If you like fashion, you want to have the newest styles.
	style [staɪl]	Stil	Do you like this style? It's very cool this year.
SB	to **wear** [weə]	(Kleidung) tragen	Sarah is wearing a pink dress.
1	**a few** [ə 'fju:]	einige	⟷ a lot
	baggy ['bægɪ]	sehr weit	⟷ tight
	to **burst** [bɜ:st]	(herein)platzen	to come in quickly
	college ['kɒlɪdʒ]	Berufs(fach)schule	A lot of young people go to college after they leave school.
	to **describe** [dɪ'skraɪb]	beschreiben	Look at the house in the picture. Then describe it.
	everybody ['evrɪˌbɒdɪ]	alle, jeder	All of the people; ⟷ nobody
	to **have to** ['hæv tə]	müssen	What homework have we got today?
	in sight [ɪn 'saɪt]	in Sicht, zu sehen	When you can see someone, they are in sight.
	jewellery ['dʒu:əlrɪ]	Schmuck	Rings and earrings are jewellery.
	to **look like** ['lʊk laɪk]	aussehen wie	James looks like his brother, Peter.
	Ms [mɪz]	Frau (auch für Unverheiratete)	When you don't know if a woman is married, you use 'Ms'.
	parking space ['pɑ:kɪŋ ˌspeɪs]	Parkplatz	where you can park your car
	personal style [ˌpɜ:sənl 'staɪl]	persönlicher Stil	what you like to wear
	problem ['prɒbləm]	Problem	"Oh, I'm sorry." – "No problem."
	second-hand [ˌseknd 'hænd]	gebraucht	A second-hand car is cheaper than a new one.
	secretary ['sekrətrɪ]	Sekretärin	A secretary works in an office.
	to **stand around** [ˌstænd ə'raʊnd]	herumstehen	He stood around and didn´t know what to do.
	student ['stju:dənt]	Schüler/in	a person who goes to college
	tight [taɪt]	eng	⟷ baggy
	What about ...? [wɒt‿ə'baʊt]	Was ist mit ...?	What about David? Is he okay?
1B	**clothes** [kləʊðz]	Bekleidung	T-shirts, jeans and skirts are clothes.
	someone ['sʌmwʌn]	jemand	= somebody
	something ['sʌmθɪŋ]	etwas	I want something to eat. Can I have some bread?
	waitress ['weɪtrɪs]	Bedienung	A waitress brings you your meal in a restaurant.
2B	**blouse** [blaʊz]	Bluse	Women wear blouses.
	leg [leg]	Bein	A dog has got four legs.
	overalls ['əʊvərɔ:lz]	Overall	A car mechanic wears overalls.
	skirt [skɜ:t]	Rock	Sarah wears skirts in summer.
	tie [taɪ]	Schlips, Krawatte	You don't wear a tie with a t-shirt.
	tights [taɪts]	Strumpfhose	When you wear a skirt in winter, you wear tights, too.
	trousers ['traʊzəz]	Hose	Donna is wearing new trousers.
	watch [wɒtʃ]	(Armband-)Uhr	I haven't got a watch. What time is it?
3A	to **brush** [brʌʃ]	bürsten	After meals you brush your teeth.
	to **look at** ['lʊk‿ət]	ansehen	Look at that picture.

Symbole: ⟷ opposite ⟶ word family = synonym

Unit 3

	perfume ['pɜ:fju:m]	Parfüm	I put on perfume before I go out.
	to **test** [test]	testen	They tested her English.
	to **try on** [traɪ‿'ɒn]	anprobieren	That's a nice t-shirt, Lisa. Why don't you try it on?
4	**driving test** ['draɪvɪŋ ˌtest]	Führerscheinprüfung	When you pass your test, you get a driving licence.
	luck [lʌk]	Glück	You can have good or bad luck.
	not ... until [nɒt ... ʌn'tɪl]	nicht ... vor	I can't go out until the weekend.
	to **make fun of** [ˌmeɪk 'fʌn‿əv]	hänseln, aufziehen	fun ⟶ to make fun of someone
	still [stɪl]	(immer) noch	Is Lisa twelve? – No, she's still eleven.
	to **take a test** [ˌteɪk ə 'test]	eine Prüfung machen	= to do a test
	umbrella [ʌm'brelə]	Regenschirm	When it rains, an umbrella keeps you dry.
	to **wish** [wɪʃ]	wünschen	I wish you a "Merry Christmas".
5	**just now** [ˌdʒʌst 'naʊ]	jetzt gerade	= at the moment
	See you then! [ˌsi: ju: 'ðen]	Bis dann!	= See you later!
	to **tidy up** [ˌtaɪdɪ‿'ʌp]	aufräumen	Now that he has tidied up his room, it looks much better.
7C	**earring** ['ɪərɪŋ]	Ohrring	Do you like the blue earrings?
	pony tail ['pəʊnɪteɪl]	zusammengebundene Haare (Zopf)	a hairstyle for long hair
	ring [rɪŋ]	Ring	He gave her a ring.
7HV	**What kind of ...?** [wɒt 'kaɪnd əv]	Was für ...?	What kind of person is she? – She's friendly.
8	**blood** [blʌd]	Blut	I've cut my finger. Look at all the blood!
	to **cut** [kʌt]	schneiden	My mother cuts my hair.
	painless ['peɪnləs]	schmerzlos	pain ⟶ painless
	piercing [pɪəsɪŋ]	Piercing	My mother doesn't like my piercing!
	professional [prə'feʃənl]	professionell	Jane is very professional in her job.
	to **staple** ['steɪpl]	tackern	You can staple papers together.
	tattoo [tæt'u:]	Tätowierung	Adam has got a tattoo of his girlfriend's name.

Unit 4

SA	**anyway** ['enɪweɪ]	außerdem, überhaupt	Smoking is expensive. It is not good for you anyway.
	garage ['gærɑ:ʒ]	Autowerkstatt	They can work on your car in the garage.
	India ['ɪndɪə]	Indien	India is a country in the east.
	skin [skɪn]	Haut	When the weather is sunny, my skin goes brown.
	without [wɪ'ðaʊt]	ohne	You mustn't go on the bus without a ticket.
SB	**for yourself** [fə jɔ:'self]	für dich (selbst)	myself, yourself, himself, herself, ourselves, yourselves, themselves
	non-smoker [ˌnɒn'sməʊkə]	Nichtraucher/in	someone who does not smoke
	racism ['reɪsɪzm]	Rassismus	We must stop racism.
1	to **become** [bɪ'kʌm]	werden	'To become' does not mean 'bekommen'.
	boss [bɒs]	Chef	I will ask the boss for more money.
	both [bəʊθ]	beide	Robert and David both like football.
	company ['kʌmpənɪ]	Firma	My mum works for an American company.
	to **earn** [ɜ:n]	verdienen	Mrs Jones has got a good job. She earns a lot of money.
	even more [ˌi:vn 'mɔ:]	noch mehr	Jane likes school, but she like holidays even more.
	fast [fɑ:st]	schnell	⟷ slow
	hard [hɑ:d]	hart	⟷ easy
	to **lose** [lu:z]	verlieren	⟷ to find
	nervous ['nɜ:vəs]	nervös	⟷ relaxed

Symbole: ⟷ opposite ⟶ word family = synonym

Unit 4

	not … anything [nɒt 'eniθɪŋ]	nichts	He didn't like anything about his job.
	of course [əv 'kɔ:s]	natürlich	Can you play football? – Of course, I can!
	on time [ɒn 'taɪm]	pünktlich	⟷ late
	over ['əʊvə]	vorbei	When this year is over, I will stop smoking.
	painter ['peɪntə]	Maler	a person who paints houses
	practical ['præktɪkl]	praktisch	I like practical hobbies so I work on my car at the weekend.
	soon [su:n]	bald	See you soon!
	tired ['taɪəd]	müde	I don't want to watch TV. I'm tired.
	to **train** [treɪn]	ausgebildet werden	Pat wants to train as a mechanic.
	trouble ['trʌbl]	Ärger, Probleme	⟷ problems
	university [ˌju:nɪ'vɜ:sətɪ]	Universität	When she left school, she went to Oxford University.
1A	to **be late** [bɪ ˌleɪt]	zu spät kommen	Sam is often late for school.
2	**advantage** [əd'vɑ:ntɪdʒ]	Vorteil	⟷ disadvantage; The advantage of a college qualification is that you can get a good job.
	to **concentrate** ['kɒntsntreɪt]	sich konzentrieren	If you don't concentrate, you will make mistakes.
	disadvantage [ˌdɪsəd'vɑ:ntɪdʒ]	Nachteil	⟷ advantage; The disadvantage of college is that you don't earn money.
	to **go wrong** [gəʊ 'rɒŋ]	schief gehen	⟷ to go right
	to **happen** ['hæpn]	passieren	It's dark in here – what's happening?
	interested ['ɪntrəstɪd]	interessiert	I'm interested in computers.
	possibility [ˌpɒsə'bɪlətɪ]	Möglichkeit	I don't like any of the possibilities.
	to **smile** ['smaɪl]	lächeln	Be friendly and smile at people!
	to **wake someone up** [weɪk ˌsʌmwʌn 'ʌp]	jemanden wecken	My alarm clock woke me up at 7 o´clock this morning.
3	to **fall in love** [ˌfɔ:l‿ɪn 'lʌv]	sich verlieben	Joanne fell in love with Paris.
	to **get married** [get 'mærɪd]	heiraten	The Burtons got married 15 years ago.
3C	**swimming** ['swɪmɪŋ]	Schwimmen	David and Simon went swimming.
4A	to **post** [pəʊst]	abschicken	= to send a letter
4B	**project** ['prɒdʒekt]	Projekt	This week we are doing a German project.
	Thanks a lot! [ˌθæŋks‿ə 'lɒt]	Vielen Dank!	= Thanks very much!
5	**abused** [ə'bju:zd]	missbraucht	Where can you get help for abused children?
	addicted [ə'dɪktɪd]	abhängig	Jack watches TV all the time. He's addicted to TV.
	badly treated [ˌbædlɪ 'tri:tɪd]	misshandelt	The dog was badly treated.
	to **be worried** [bɪ 'wʌrɪd]	sich Sorgen machen	= to worry
	drug [drʌg]	Droge	Cigarettes are drugs, too.
	emergency number [ɪ'mɜ:dʒənsɪ ˌnʌmbə]	Notruf	You call an emergency number to get the police.
	to **run away** [rʌn‿ə'weɪ]	weglaufen	She ran away from home last month. The police helped her to call home.
	to **steal** [sti:l]	stehlen	Robin Hood stole money from people who had too much money.
	terrible ['terəbl]	schrecklich	⟷ great
	unhappy [ʌn'hæpɪ]	unglücklich	⟷ happy; = sad
5C	**consequence** ['kɒnsɪkwəns]	Konsequenz, Folge	Think about the consequences before you do something!
5HV	to **fit** [fɪt]	passen	The new trousers fitted him well.
	to **get caught** [get 'kɔ:t]	erwischt werden	He was caught when he took a pullover from a shop.
	to **kick someone off** [kɪk ˌsʌmwʌn 'ɒf]	jemanden rausschmeißen	The trainer didn't want Joe to play so he kicked him off the team.
	pill [pɪl]	Tablette, Pille	When you are ill, you can take pills.

Symbole: ⟷ opposite ⟶ word family = synonym

Unit 5

S	**kind** [kaɪnd]	Art	What kind of music do you like, David?
	media ['miːdɪə]	Medien	Television and radio are media.
	probably ['prɒbəblɪ]	wahrscheinlich	They're playing very well today. They'll probably win.
1	**album** ['ælbəm]	Album	Katie's album was a big hit in Britain.
	to **appear** [ə'pɪə]	Gast sein	My aunt has appeared on a TV show.
	Belfast [bel'fɑːst]	Stadt in Nordirland	Belfast is the capital of Northern Ireland.
	born [bɔːn]	geboren	My baby brother was born on Sunday.
	to **bring out** [brɪŋ 'aʊt]	herausbringen	= to release
	Britain ['brɪtn]	Großbritannien	Britain ⟶ British
	Brit College for Performing Arts [ˌbrɪt 'kɒlɪdʒ fə pəˌfɔːmɪŋ 'ɑːts]	Musik- und Schauspielschule in England	This is a college where you can learn to sing or play an instrument.
	charity ['tʃærɪtɪ]	wohltätiger Zweck	The school made money for a charity in their town.
	to **discover** [dɪ'skʌvə]	entdecken	They discovered that she could sing when she was eight.
	future ['fjuːtʃə]	Zukunft	past – present – future
	Georgia ['dʒɔːdʒə]	Georgien	Georgia is a country in eastern Europe.
	hit [hɪt]	Hit	Blueday has had many hits in America.
	to **move** [muːv]	umziehen	to leave your home and go to live in another town.
	producer [prə'djuːsə]	Produzent	someone who finds singers for record labels
	star [stɑː]	Star	Some pop stars also become film stars.
	successful [sək'sesfʊl]	erfolgreich	If you work hard, you will be successful.
	through [θruː]	durch	You can look through a window.
	whatever [wɒt'evə]	was auch immer	Whatever you do after school, you must work hard.
1D	**Burma** ['bɜːmə]	Birma	Burma is a country in the east.
	Israel ['ɪzreɪəl]	Israel	Israel is a country in the east.
	pub [pʌb]	Kneipe	a place where you can have a drink and meet friends
2	**DVD shop** [ˌdiːviː'diː ˌʃɒp]	DVD Verleih	a place where you can get DVDs
	newsagent's ['njuːzˌeɪdʒənts]	Zeitungskiosk	a place where you can buy magazines
	next to [nekst‿tuː]	neben	Tom is standing next to Susie.
	to **own** [əʊn]	besitzen	This is our house. = We own it.
	owner ['əʊnə]	Besitzer/in	owner ⟶ to own
	row [rəʊ]	Reihe	We have tickets for the cinema. We are going to sit in row 9.
3	to **switch on** [swɪtʃ‿'ɒn]	einschalten	When you switch on the TV, the picture comes on.
4	**press release** ['pres rɪˌliːs]	Pressemitteilung	information given to journalists
	record label ['rekɔːd ˌleɪbl]	Plattenfirma	the name of a record company
	release [rɪ'liːs]	Neuerscheinung	"Now we'll listen to Katie Melua's newest release!"
	to **release** [rɪ'liːs]	herausbringen	= to bring out
	tour [tʊə]	Tournee	How long is Blueday's tour of Germany? – It's one week.
5	**violent** ['vaɪələnt]	gewalttätig	The film was very violent but we enjoyed it.
7	**soap** [səʊp]	Seifenoper	My mum watches all of the TV soaps.

Symbole: ⟷ opposite ⟶ word family = synonym

Unit 6

S	**guide** [gaɪd]	Reiseführer	a person who gives you information about a city or a sight
	lift [lɪft]	Aufzug	In every good hotel you can take a lift to get upstairs or downstairs.
	rush hour ['rʌʃ ˌaʊə]	Hauptverkehrszeit	the time before work in the morning and after work in the afternoon when many people are on the roads
	stop and go traffic [ˌstɒpəngəʊ 'træfɪk]	stockender Verkehr	When the street is crowded with cars, there is only stop and go traffic.
1	**all night** [ˌɔ:l 'naɪt]	die ganze Nacht	We had a party all night. We came home in the morning.
	continent ['kɒntɪnənt]	Kontinent	Europe is a continent.
	crowded ['kraʊdɪd]	voll (mit Menschen)	The shopping centre is crowded with people.
	delicious [dɪ'lɪʃəs]	lecker	I love this cake. It's delicious.
	double-decker [ˌdʌbl 'dekə]	Doppeldecker-	In London many buses are double-deckers.
	flea market ['fli:ˌmɑ:kɪt]	Flohmarkt	On Sundays there is a flea market in the car park.
	to **go sightseeing** [ˌgəʊ 'saɪtsi:ɪŋ]	Sehenswürdigkeiten anschauen	When you go sightseeing in London, you visit Tower Bridge and Buckingham Palace.
	low [ləʊ]	niedrig	⟷ high
	one-day travelcard [ˌwʌndeɪ 'trævl ˌkɑ:d]	Tagesfahrkarte	a ticket for one day
	per [pɜ:]	pro	Fast trains can travel at 300 km per hour.
	pocket money ['pɒkɪt ˌmʌnɪ]	Taschengeld	Children get pocket money from their parents.
	thought [θɔ:t]	Gedanke	to think ⟶ a thought
	vegetarian [ˌvedʒɪ'teərɪən]	vegetarisch	No hamburgers, thanks. I'm a vegetarian.
	wax model [ˌwæks 'mɒdl]	Wachsfigur	At Madam Tussaud's you can see wax models of Madonna and Robbie Williams.
	YHA [ˌwaɪeɪtʃ'eɪ]	Jugendherbergsvereinigung	All of the youth hostels in Britain are in the YHA.
	youth hostel ['ju:θ ˌhɒstl]	Jugendherberge	On our class trip we stayed at a youth hostel.
4	**enough** [ɪ'nʌf]	genug	I don't have enough money to buy a big car.
	to **lend** [lend]	leihen	If you lend money, you give money to someone but you want to have it back one day.
	mile [maɪl]	Meile (ca. 1,6 km)	A mile is 1,609 metres long.
	to **pack** [pæk]	(zusammen)packen	You pack your things in a bag before you go on holiday.
	receptionist [rɪ'sepʃənɪst]	Dame / Herr am Empfang	The receptionist at the hotel can give you information about London.
	to **wait** [weɪt]	warten	Please, wait for me. I'll be there in five minutes.
7HV	**breakdown** ['breɪkdaʊn]	Panne	My car had a breakdown. I had to call a garage.
	delay [dɪ'leɪ]	Verspätung	The plane has a delay of one hour.
	direction [dɪ'rekʃn]	Richtung	If you want to visit the market, you must go in this direction.
	engine ['endʒɪn]	Maschine, Motor	Many cars have the engine in front of the driver.
	ferry ['ferɪ]	Fähre	You go from Calais to Dover by ferry.
	flight [flaɪt]	Flug	to fly ⟶ flight A flight is a trip by plane.
	snow [snəʊ]	Schnee	Rain in summer – snow in winter.
7B	**means of transport** [ˌmi:nz‿əv 'træntspɔ:t]	Verkehrsmittel	Cars, buses and planes are all means of transport.
	passenger ['pæsndʒə]	Passagiere	A person who goes by plane, train or car but who is not the driver.
8	to **change** [tʃeɪndʒ]	umsteigen	Does this train go to London? – No, it only goes as far as Birmingham. Then we have to change.

Symbole: ⟷ opposite ⟶ word family = synonym

Unit 7

SB	to **grow up** [grəʊ͜ˈʌp]	erwachsen werden	= to become an adult
	sick [sɪk]	krank	"I feel sick!"
SHV	to **guess** [ges]	raten, schätzen	I've no idea what it is. – Well, guess what it is!
	to **have (got) the nerve** [ˌhæv ðə ˈnɜːv; həv ˌgɒt͜ ðə ˈnɜːv]	die Frechheit haben	He has got the nerve to think that he is better than me.
	to **turn red** [tɜːn ˈred]	rot werden	I turn red when I go out in the sun.
SD	**afraid** [əˈfreɪd]	ängstlich	The child was afraid of dogs.
	frustrated [frʌsˈtreɪtɪd]	frustriert	The singer is frustrated about the problem.
	worried [ˈwʌrɪd]	besorgt	to worry ⟶ worried
1A	**at least** [ət ˈliːst]	wenigstens	He has got at least three or four mobile phones.
	by bus [baɪ ˈbʌs]	mit dem Bus	by bus, by plane, by train; on foot
	driving licence [ˈdraɪvɪŋ ˌlaɪsəns]	Führerschein	You can get a driving licence when you are eighteen.
	fantastic [fænˈtæstɪk]	fantastisch	= great; ⟷ terrible; Surfing is fantastic.
	German [ˈdʒɜːmən]	deutsch	Kevin is German and he speaks German. But he hasn't got a German name.
	Germany [ˈdʒɜːmənɪ]	Deutschland	Germany ⟶ German
	to **get there** [ˈget͜ ðeə]	hinkommen	Can you come to my party? Yes, but I can't get there before eight o' clock.
	Indian [ˈɪndɪən]	indisch	Mrs Brooks comes from India, so she cooks Indian food.
	lunchtime [ˈlʌntʃtaɪm]	mittags	I usually eat a sandwich at lunchtime.
	meal [miːl]	Essen	Breakfast and lunch are meals.
	to **miss** [mɪs]	vermissen	My older brothers live in another town now so I miss them a lot.
	not … at all [nɒt … ət ˈɔːl]	überhaupt nicht	She doesn't like ground beef at all.
	peanut butter cookie [ˌpiːnʌtˌbʌtə ˈkʊkɪ]	Ernussbutterkeks	Peanut butter cookies come from America.
	Russia [ˈrʌʃə]	Russland	Russia is in the east of Europe.
	Russian pancake [ˌrʌʃən ˈpænkeɪk]	russischer Pfannkuchen	Blinis are Russian pancakes.
	So what? [ˌsəʊ͜ˈwɒt]	Ja und?	I forgot to bring your CD back. – So what? You can bring it on Monday.
	tonight [təˈnaɪt]	heute Abend	We're going to a concert tonight. It starts at seven o'clock.
	Turkish [ˈtɜːkɪʃ]	türkisch	Köfte are Turkish meatballs.
1C	to **invite** [ɪnˈvaɪt]	einladen	to invite ⟶ invitation
2	to **add** [æd]	hinzufügen	Add some salt to the cooking water.
	breadcrumbs [ˈbredkrʌmz]	Paniermehl	You don't need breadcrumbs for Turkish meatballs.
	to **check the seasoning** [ˌtʃek ðə ˈsiːzənɪŋ]	abschmecken	Check the seasoning before you finish cooking the meal.
	egg [eg]	Ei	You need three eggs for this cake.
	flat [flæt]	flach	American meatballs are flat.
	ground beef [ˌgraʊnd͜ˈbiːf]	Rinderhackfleisch	Anne doesn't eat ground beef. She's a vegetarian.
	to **heat** [hiːt]	erhitzen	This meal is cold. Can you heat it, please?
	lb [paʊnd]	Abkürzung für Pfund (453,6 g)	There is 1lb of flour in the cake.
	to **mix** [mɪks]	vermischen	Mix the ground beef and breadcrumbs.
	porcupine [ˈpɔːkjəpaɪn]	Stachelschwein	The porcupine meatballs don't look like a real porcupine.
	pot [pɒt]	Topf	You heat the water in a pot.
	raw [rɔː]	ungekocht	The meat is raw! You must cook it more.
	recipe [ˈresɪpɪ]	(Koch-)Rezept	I have a good recipe for chocolate cookies.

Symbole: ⟷ opposite ⟶ word family = synonym

Unit 7

	rice [raɪs]	Reis	Would you like chips or rice? – Rice, please.
	to **roll** [rəʊl]	rollen	Roll the ground beef into balls.
	salt [sɔ:lt; sɒlt]	Salz	This meal is terrible! There is too much salt.
	sauce [sɔ:s]	Soße	I love ice cream with chocolate sauce.
	to **simmer** ['sɪmə]	köcheln	The meatballs simmer in the tomato sauce.
	teaspoon ['ti:spu:n]	Teelöffel	A teaspoon of paprika is too much. Half a teaspoon is enough.
2A	**onion** ['ʌnjən]	Zwiebel	Cut the onion into small pieces.
4A	**Africa** ['æfrɪka]	Afrika	Many countries in Africa are poor.
	to **accept** [ək'sept]	akzeptieren	I am happy to accept your help with this project.
	as … as [əz … əz]	so … wie	I will finish my homework as quickly as possible.
	hundreds ['hʌndrədz]	Hunderte	He knows hundreds of songs.
	language ['læŋgwɪdʒ]	Sprache	English and Turkish are languages.
	possible ['pɒsəbl]	möglich	possibility ⟶ possible
	world [wɜ:ld]	Welt	America is in a different part of the world from us.
5	**passport** ['pɑ:spɔ:t]	Reisepass	Donna is from England so she has a British passport.
	relaxed [rɪ'lækst]	locker	⟷ nervous
	Turkey ['tɜ:kɪ]	Türkei	Tarik's grandmother lives in Turkey.
6HV	**elective** [ɪ'lektɪv]	Wahlfach	An elective is a subject that you can choose.
	practice ['præktɪs]	Übung; Training	practice ⟶ to practise
	quarter ['kwɔ:tə]	Schulsemester	The first quarter begins in September.
	required course [rɪˌkwaɪəd 'kɔ:s]	Pflichtfach	English is a required course in my school.
	Spanish ['spænɪʃ]	Spanisch	People speak Spanish in Spain.
	subject ['sʌbdʒɪkt]	Fach	English and Maths are school subjects.
	to **surf** [sɜ:f]	surfen	Surfing the internet with friends is fun!
	web site ['websaɪt]	Webseite	My school has got a web site on the internet.

Unit 8

S	**best-known** [ˌbest‿'nəʊn]	bekannteste	Robbie Williams is one of the best-known singers in England.
	east [i:st]	östlich	Wales is east of Ireland.
	Europe ['jʊərəp]	Europa	England and Germany are in Europe, but Canada is not.
	Great Britain [ˌgreɪt‿'brɪtn]	Großbritannien	England, Scotland and Wales are all in Great Britain.
	north [nɔ:θ]	nördlich	⟷ south; Hamburg is north of Berlin.
	northern ['nɔ:ðn]	Nord-	Hamburg is in northern Germany.
	republic [rɪ'pʌblɪk]	Republik	Germany has no king or queen. It is a republic.
	Scotland ['skɒtlənd]	Schottland	Scotland is in the north of England.
	south [saʊθ]	südlich	Stuttgart is south of Mannheim.
	United Kingdom (UK) [ju:ˌnaɪtɪd 'kɪŋdəm]	Vereinigtes Königreich	The United Kingdom is the name for Great Britain and Northern Ireland.
	Wales [weɪlz]	Wales	Wales is west of England.
	west [west]	westlich	⟷ east
1	**Brit** [brɪt]	Brite, Britin	= a person who lives in Britain
	difference ['dɪfrnts]	Unterschied	different ⟶ difference
	exchange [ɪks'tʃeɪndʒ]	Austausch	In an exchange between schools in different countries, pupils and teachers visit each other's schools.
	fishing ['fɪʃɪŋ]	Fischerei	to fish ⟶ a fish ⟶ fishing

Symbole: ⟷ opposite ⟶ word family = synonym

Unit 8

	fun [fʌn]	Spaß	It's fun to play basketball!
	joke [dʒəʊk]	Witz	something that you say to make people laugh
	motor racing ['məʊtə ˌreɪsɪŋ]	Autorennen	Many people watch motor racing at Silverstone.
	port [pɔ:t]	Hafen	You can see big ships in the port of Hamburg.
	trendsetter ['trendˌsetə]	Trendsetter	a person who starts a new fashion or trend
	vocational [vəʊ'keɪʃənl]	Berufs-, beruflich	If you want to learn a job, you must do vocational training.
	world-class [ˌwɜ:ld'klɑ:s]	Weltklasse	A world-class car is one of the best cars in the world.
1C	**excellent** ['eksələnt]	ausgezeichnet	= very good
2	**cereal** ['sɪərɪəl]	Frühstücksgetreide	You have cereal with milk for breakfast.
	cheerful(ly) ['tʃɪəfʊl, 'tʃɪəfʊlɪ]	fröhlich	= happy, happily
	to **deliver** [dɪ'lɪvə]	liefern	to take something to a place
	diary ['daɪərɪ]	Tagebuch	a book where you write what has happened each day
	DIY (Do It Yourself) [ˌdi:aɪ'waɪ (ˌdʊɪtjə'self)]	Heimwerker-	If you want to repair something at home, you first go to the DIY centre and buy the things that you need.
	milkman ['mɪlkmən]	Milchmann	a person who brings milk to a lot of British houses every morning
	regular(ly) ['regjələ, 'regjələlɪ]	regelmäßig	It happens again and again at the same time. The milkman comes regularly.
4	**husband** ['hʌzbənd]	Ehemann	⟷ wife
	invitation [ˌɪnvɪ'teɪʃn]	Einladung	⟶ to invite; I've got an invitation to a party on Saturday.
4HV	**anyone** ['enɪwʌn]	(irgend)jemand	= any person; Did anyone see the accident?
	to **believe** [bɪ'li:v]	glauben	Many people believe in God.
	costs [kɒsts]	Kosten	money that you have to pay for something
	to **fetch** [fetʃ]	(ab)holen	to go and get something
	free [fri:]	frei	It's free! You needn't pay for it.
	guardian angel [ˌgɑ:dɪən 'eɪndʒl]	Schutzengel	When you do bungee jumping, you need a guardian angel.
	speed limit ['spi:d ˌlɪmɪt]	Geschwindigkeits-begrenzung	Don't drive too fast! There's a speed limit of 50 miles an hour.
4B	to **mean** [mi:n]	bedeuten	What does 'kindergarten' mean?
5	**necessary** ['nesəsrɪ]	nötig	It won't be necessary to book a table in the restaurant. = You won't need to book a table.
	typical ['tɪpɪkl]	typisch	a good example of something; That's typical of you!

Unit 9

S	**artist** ['ɑ:tɪst]	Künstler/in	someone who paints pictures or makes music
	at the back [ət‿ðə 'bæk]	hinten	⟷ at the front
	at the front [ət‿ðə 'frʌnt]	vorne	⟷ at the back
	bridge [brɪdʒ]	Brücke	A bridge goes over a river.
	factory ['fæktrɪ]	Fabrik	a large building where things are made
	hill [hɪl]	Hügel	A hill is smaller than a mountain.
	in the middle [ɪn ðə 'mɪdl]	in der Mitte, mitten in	It is not at the back, it is not at the front – it is in the middle.
	lorry ['lɒrɪ]	LKW, Lastwagen	You use a lorry to carry heavy things.
	plane [pleɪn]	Flugzeug	He went to New York by plane.
	traffic lights ['træfɪk ˌlaɪts]	Verkehrsampel	lights in the streets that change from green to yellow and red

Symbole: ⟷ opposite ⟶ word family = synonym

Unit 9

1	**already** [ɔ:l'redɪ]	schon	Have you got this CD? – Yes, I've already got it.
	area ['eərɪə]	Gegend	= part of a country
	to **attract** [ə'trækt]	anziehen	to make someone want to come nearer
	compost ['kɒmpɒst]	Kompost	Compost helps vegetables to grow better.
	cucumber ['kju:kʌmbə]	Salatgurke	a long, green vegetable
	customer ['kʌstəmə]	Kunde, Kundin	A customer buys things in a shop.
	dangerous ['deɪndʒrəs]	gefährlich	Don't go so fast – it's dangerous.
	dealer ['di:lə]	Händler/in, Dealer	A dealer buys and sells drugs.
	dirty ['dɜ:tɪ]	schmutzig	↔ clean
	to **get rid of** [get 'rɪd‿əv]	loswerden	If you have something you do not like, you get rid of it.
	to **impress** [ɪm'pres]	beeindrucken	At work I hoped to impress my new boss.
	local ['ləʊkl]	aus der Gegend, örtlich	The schools in your area are your local schools.
	to **move out** [mu:v 'aʊt]	aus-, wegziehen	to leave a house where you lived
	to **pollute** [pə'lu:t, pə'lju:t]	(Umwelt) verschmutzen	If you pollute water, you make it dirty.
	revolution [ˌrevə'lu:ʃn]	Revolution	The French Revolution was in 1789.
	smell [smel]	Geruch	There's a smell of flowers in the air.
	vegetable ['vedʒtəbl]	Gemüse	The Millers eat lots of vegetables from their garden.
1D	**carrot** ['kærət]	Karotte	a long, orange vegetable
	to **grow** [grəʊ]	wachsen	Trees grow in our garden.
	potato [pə'teɪtəʊ]	Kartoffel	Potatoes are round vegetables that grow in the earth.
2	**lead** [li:d]	Leine	You must keep your dog on a lead in the street.
	own [əʊn]	eigene(r)	I have got my own bedroom.
3B	**main** [meɪn]	Haupt-	= most important
	noise [nɔɪz]	Lärm, Krach	Don't make so much noise! = Don't be so loud!
	noisy ['nɔɪzɪ]	laut	= loud
	to **offer** ['ɒfə]	(an-)bieten	Can I offer you a drink? = Would you like a drink?
4	**bread roll** [ˌbred 'rəʊl]	kleines weiches Brötchen	Would you like bread rolls for breakfast?
	crisps [krɪsps]	(Kartoffel-)Chips	Many people like crisps with salt or with cheese and onion.
	fork [fɔ:k]	Gabel	You need a fork to eat noodles.
	knife, knives [naɪf, naɪvz]	Messer	You need a knife to cut bread.
	orange juice ['ɒrɪndʒ ˌdʒu:s]	Orangensaft	a drink which is made from oranges
	peanut ['pi:nʌt]	Erdnuss	In the USA people like peanut butter on toast.
	plate [pleɪt]	Teller	When you eat, you put your food on a plate.
	salad ['sæləd]	(angemachter) Salat	a meal of cold, raw vegetables
	spoon [spu:n]	Löffel	You eat soup with a spoon.
5HV	**apartment** [ə'pɑ:tmənt]	(US) Wohnung	apartment (US) = flat (BE)
	glad [glæd]	froh	= happy
	nature ['neɪtʃə]	Natur	all of the animals and plants in the world
	to **save** [seɪv]	sparen	You can save money or time.
	simple ['sɪmpl]	einfach	= easy
6	**church** [tʃɜ:tʃ]	Kirche	We go to church on Sunday.
	cow [kaʊ]	Kuh	a big farm animal which gives milk
	except [ɪk'sept]	außer	Everybody is here, except Jenny.
	to **grow** [grəʊ]	anpflanzen	We grow vegetables in our garden.
	to **produce** [prə'dju:s]	produzieren	= to make
	railway ['reɪlweɪ]	Bahnlinie	You can hear the trains. There is a railway near here.

Symbole: ↔ opposite ⟶ word family = synonym

Unit 10

S	**Austria** ['ɒstrɪə]	Österreich	a country between Italy and Germany
	Belgium ['beldʒəm]	Belgien	the country between the Netherlands and France
	Greece [gri:s]	Griechenland	a country in southeast Europe
	Portugal ['pɔ:tʃʊgəl]	Portugal	the country west of Spain
	Spain [speɪn]	Spanien	the country between Portugal and France
	Switzerland ['swɪtsələnd]	die Schweiz	the country between France and Italy
	the Netherlands [ðə 'neðələndz]	die Niederlande	the country north of Belgium
SB	**capital** ['kæpɪtl]	Hauptstadt	London is the capital of England.
1	**by the way** [ˌbaɪ ðə 'weɪ]	übrigens	You say "by the way" when you add something that you have just thought of.
	campsite ['kæmpsaɪt]	Zeltplatz	When you go camping, you stay on a campsite.
	expensive [ɪk'spentsɪv]	teuer	⟷ cheap
	InterRail ['ɪntəreɪl]	InterRail (Zugreisen zu Sonderkonditionen)	Young people can get cheap Interrail tickets.
	It was real fun! [ɪt‿wəz ˌrɪəl 'fʌn]	Es hat echt Spaß gemacht!	= We enjoyed it.
	most of all ['məʊst‿əv‿ˌɔ:l]	am besten, am meisten	More than other things.
	Sounds good! [ˌsaʊndz 'gʊd]	Hört sich gut an!	= That's a good idea!
	weather ['weðə]	Wetter	What's the weather like? – It's raining.
1B	**fare** [feə]	Fahrpreis	money that you pay when you go by bus or train
2A	**favourite** ['feɪvrɪt]	liebste/r/s	I like basketball and I like tennis, too. But my favourite sport is football.
3	**fishing** ['fɪʃɪŋ]	Angeln	When you go fishing, you try to catch fish.
	to **give up (smoking)** [gɪv 'ʌp (ˌsməʊkɪŋ)]	(das Rauchen) aufgeben	= to stop (smoking)
	not ... yet [nɒt ... jet]	noch nicht	Where is Tom? – He has not arrived yet.
	to **prefer** [prɪ'fɜ:]	vorziehen	= to like more/better
	sailing ['seɪlɪŋ]	Segeln	You need wind if you want to go sailing.
4	**as** [æz]	da, weil	= because
	to **cross** [krɒs]	überqueren	Look left, then right, then left. Then cross the road.
	difficulty ['dɪfɪkəltɪ]	Schwierigkeit	= problem
	sights [saɪts]	Sehenswürdigkeiten	Tower Bridge and Buckingham Palace are interesting sights.
	such a ['sʌtʃ‿ə]	solch ein/e/r	Sandra's such a nice girl!
	traffic ['træfɪk]	Verkehr	There are a lot of cars on the road. = There is a lot of traffic.
	useful ['ju:sfl]	nützlich	You can often use a pocket knife. So it's useful.
5HV	to **book** [bʊk]	reservieren, buchen	You can book a ticket or a holiday or a table in a restaurant.
	non-smoking [ˌnɒn'sməʊkɪŋ]	Nichtraucher-	A non-smoking restaurant is a place where you mustn't smoke.
	overnight [ˌəʊvə'naɪt]	über Nacht	If you stay overnight, you stay until the next day.
	pet [pet]	Haustier	an animal that you keep in your house or garden
	platform ['plætfɔ:m]	Bahnsteig	Which is the platform for the train to London?
	reservation [ˌrezə'veɪʃn]	Reservierung	I have got a reservation for a seat in the train.
	seat [si:t]	(Sitz-)Platz	the place where you sit in a train, a plane or the theatre
6	**Australian** [ɒs'treɪlɪən]	australisch	Australian tourists must travel a long time to visit Europe.
6HV	to **arrange** [ə'reɪndʒ]	arrangieren, besorgen	If you want a ticket for the football match, I can arrange to buy it for you.

Symbole: ⟷ opposite ⟶ word family = synonym

Unit 10

to **be delighted** [bɪ dɪ'laɪtɪd]	sich freuen	= to be very happy
gentleman ['dʒentlmən]	Herr	man ⟷ woman; gentleman ⟷ lady
inhabitant [ɪn'hæbɪtənt]	Einwohner/in	someone who lives in a place
known ['nəʊn]	bekannt	It is known = People know it.
lady ['leɪdɪ]	Dame	woman ⟷ man; lady ⟷ gentleman
to **pass** [pɑ:s]	vorbei fahren / gehen	On our tour of London we passed Buckingham Palace. We didn't stop.
while [waɪl]	während	Terry phoned me while I was working.

Unit 11

S	**disk drive** ['dɪsk‿draɪv]	Diskettenlaufwerk	The computer can read the diskette if you put it into the disk drive.
	DVD burner [ˌdi:vi:'di: ˌbɜ:nə]	DVD-Brenner	A DVD burner can copy a DVD.
	DVD drive [ˌdi:vi:'di: ˌdraɪv]	DVD-Laufwerk	A DVD drive can read a DVD.
	hard disk ['hɑ:d‿dɪsk]	Festplatte	the place inside the PC where you save information
	headset ['hedset]	Headset	You put on a headset when you want to speak to someone and to listen to someone on the internet.
	integrated modem [ˌɪntɪgreɪtɪd 'məʊdem]	integriertes Modem	It connects your PC with the internet.
	keyboard ['ki:bɔ:d]	Tastatur	You find all the letters of the alphabet and numbers on the keyboard.
	(laser) printer [(ˌleɪzə) 'prɪntə]	(Laser-)Drucker	a machine which puts letters on paper
	loudspeaker [ˌlaʊd'spi:kə]	Lautsprecher	the part of a radio or TV from which you hear music
	monitor ['mɒnɪtə]	Bildschirm	You can see pictures or texts on the monitor of a PC.
	mouse [maʊs]	Maus	It is a little grey animal – but it also helps you to work on the PC.
	scanner ['skænə]	Bildabtaster, Scanner	A scanner reads written texts and you can copy them onto your hard disk.
	USB port [ˌju:es'bi: ˌpɔ:t]	USB-Port	You use a USB port to connect a camera with a PC.
	webcam ['webkæm]	Webcam	It takes pictures and sends them to other people who use the internet.
1	**as an adult** [əz‿ən 'ædʌlt]	als Erwachsener	As an adult you can do more than a child.
	to **carry out** [ˌkærɪ‿'aʊt]	ausführen	When you carry out something, you do it and you finish it.
	to **control** [kən'trəʊl]	kontrollieren, beherrschen	to have the power to make something do what you want
	guy [gaɪ]	Typ	He's a nice guy. = He's a nice man.
	he realized [hɪ 'rɪəlaɪzd]	es wurde ihm klar	= he understood, he found out
	huge [hju:dʒ]	riesig	= very big
	to **install** [ɪn'stɔ:l]	installieren, einsetzen	to put a new thing in its place
	in the late 1960s [ɪn ðə ˌleɪt ˌnaɪnti:n 'sɪkstɪz]	Ende der 60er Jahre	= 1968 or 1969
	to **last** [lɑ:st]	dauern	A day lasts 24 hours.
	move [mu:v]	(Spiel) Zug	He made a bad move and he lost the game.
	not even [nɒt‿'i:vn]	noch nicht einmal	Nobody can do that, not even Superman!
	order ['ɔ:də]	Befehl	words that tell someone to do something
	result [rɪ'zʌlt]	Ergebnis	Look, I've got the football results. Liverpool 2 – Arsenal 0.

Unit 11

	size [saɪz]	Größe	Have you got this T-shirt in a different size, please?
	software program ['sɒftweə ˌprəʊgræm]	Computerprogramm	"Microsoft Word" is a popular software program.
	to **speed up** [spiːd 'ʌp]	schneller machen	to make something go more quickly
	tic-tac-toe [ˌtɪktæk'təʊ]	Spiel	Tic-tac-toe is an easy game for two people.
	to **type in** [taɪp 'ɪn]	eintippen	When you type in letters on the keyboard, you can see them on the screen.
1B	**silent** ['saɪlənt]	leise	Everybody knows the Christmas song: "Silent night".
1C	to **print** [prɪnt]	drucken	You print a text on a piece of paper at home so that you can take it to school.
3	**cash desk** ['kæʃ ˌdesk]	Kasse	the place in a shop where you pay
	sales assistant ['seɪlz‿əˌsɪstənt]	Verkäufer/in	A sales assistant sells things in a shop.
4A	**caller** ['kɔːlə]	Anrufer/in	someone who calls you on the phone
	screen [skriːn]	Bildschirm	TVs and computers have a screen.
5	to **run a shop** [rʌn ə 'ʃɒp]	ein Geschäft leiten	The manager runs the shop.
6HV	**all over the world** [ɔːl ˌəʊvə ðə 'wɜːld]	auf der ganzen Welt	= in every country
	board [bɔːd]	Tafel	There is a board in every classroom.
	to **contact** ['kɒntækt]	Kontakt aufnehmen	When I saw the accident, I contacted the police.
	to **spend** [spend]	ausgeben	to pay money for something
7	**bill** [bɪl]	Rechnung	We'd like to pay. Can you bring us the bill, please?
	to **chat** [tʃæt]	sich unterhalten	to talk about things that are not very important
	Dear Sir [ˌdɪə 'sɜː]	(Leserbrief) Anrede	a way to start a letter (to a newspaper)
	to **download** ['daʊnləʊd]	herunterladen	You can download interesting information from the internet.
	to **hang around** [ˌhæŋ‿ə'raʊnd]	herumhängen	If you hang around, you stay in one place and don't really do anything.
	to **make up one's mind** [meɪk ˌʌp wʌnz 'maɪnd]	sich entscheiden	to decide to do something
	personnel manager [ˌpɜːsən'el ˌmænɪdʒə]	Personalchef/in	If you want to apply for a job, you must write to the personnel manager.
	skill [skɪl]	Fähigkeit, Fertigkeit	When you learn new skills, you learn how to do special kinds of work really well.
	unemployed [ˌʌnɪm'plɔɪd]	arbeitslos	When you have no work, you are unemployed.
8HV	to **close** [kləʊz]	schließen	You can close a file on your PC.
	file [faɪl]	Datei	A file is a piece of information on your PC which has its own name.
	to **format** ['fɔːmæt]	formatieren	When you format a diskette, there is no more information on it afterwards.
	to **load** [ləʊd]	laden	You can load things onto a lorry or you can load a program or file onto your PC.
	to **save** [seɪv]	speichern	You save information on the hard disk of your PC.
	to **switch off** [swɪtʃ‿'ɒf]	ausschalten	⟷ to switch on

Unit 12

1	to **apply** [ə'plaɪ]	sich bewerben	to write to ask for a job
	apprenticeship [ə'prentɪʃɪp]	Berufsausbildung, Lehre	the time when someone learns to do a job
	to **be employed** [bɪ‿ɪm'plɔɪd]	angestellt sein	= to have work; ⟷ to be unemployed, to be out of work

Symbole: ⟷ opposite ⟶ word family = synonym

Unit 12

	between [bɪ'twi:n]	zwischen	Terry is sitting between Sam and Emma.
	chance [tʃɑ:nts]	Chance, Möglichkeit	We didn't have the chance to see the Tower because we only had one hour in London.
	communication [kəˌmju:nɪ'keɪʃn]	Kommunikation	when you tell something or write something to a person
	engineering [ˌendʒɪ'nɪərɪŋ]	Technik; Maschinenbau	the job of planning and making machines
	exactly [ɪg'zæktlɪ]	genau	It's my 13th birthday today – so I'm now exactly 13 years old.
	full-time [ˌfʊl'taɪm]	Vollzeit	When you work 40 hours a week, you work full-time.
	in addition [ɪn ə'dɪʃn]	zusätzlich	When Sarah fell, she broke her arm and, in addition, she broke her glasses.
	level ['levl]	Stufe	He plays football at a very high level.
	mainly ['meɪnlɪ]	hauptsächlich	Babies mainly drink milk.
	on-the-job training [ˌɒnðədʒɒb 'treɪnɪŋ]	innerbetriebliche Ausbildung	learning about a job while you are working in a company
	paper-making ['peɪpəˌmeɪkɪŋ]	Papierherstellung	the job of producing paper
	school leaver ['sku:l‿li:və]	Schulabgänger/in	A school leaver is a person who has just finished school.
	towards [tə'wɔ:dz]	auf … zu	= in the direction of
2A	**apprentice** [ə'prentɪs]	Auszubildende/r, Lehrling	a young worker who is learning his/her job
	to **inform** [ɪn'fɔ:m]	informieren	to inform ⟶ information; to tell something to a person.
2B	**department** [dɪ'pɑ:tmənt]	Abteilung	a part of a big company
	sales [seɪlz]	Vertrieb	The sales department is the part of the company which sells the products.
	trainer ['treɪnə]	Ausbilder/in	trainer ⟶ to train; someone who teaches people a job
3	**colleague** ['kɒli:g]	Kollege, Kollegin	a person who works with you in a company
	match [mætʃ]	Spiel	= a game (of football); "Can we watch the match this evening?"
	some [sʌm]	einige	Some of the workers are on holiday today.
5HV	**advice** [əd'vaɪs]	Rat(schlag)	ein Ratschlag = some advice; Let me give you some advice.
	carpenter ['kɑ:pəntə]	Schreiner/in	a person who makes tables or chairs from wood
	course guide ['kɔ:s ˌgaɪd]	Kursübersicht	a plan of the lessons
	experience [ɪk'spɪərɪənts]	Erfahrung	knowing about things because you have done or seen them
	hairstylist ['heəˌstaɪlɪst]	Frisörin	a person whose job is to cut and style hair

Activity page 1

absolutely [ˌæbsə'lu:tlɪ]	absolut	= completely
launderette [ˌlɔ:ndr'et]	Waschsalon	You can wash your clothes in a launderette.
midnight ['mɪdnaɪt]	Mitternacht	The party began at midnight and finished at 6 o'clock in the morning.

Symbole: ⟷ opposite ⟶ word family = synonym

Activity page 3

to **climb** [klaɪm]	klettern	You can't climb a hill in those shoes!
custom ['kʌstəm]	Brauch	In Germany we have different Christmas customs to England.
to **decorate** ['dekreɪt]	schmücken	The children helped to decorate the Christmas tree.

Symbole: ↔ opposite ⟶ word family = synonym

Alphabetische Wortliste

A

a bit	ein bisschen	2/1
a few	einige	3/1
absolutely	absolut	AP/1
abused	missbraucht	4/5
to **accept**	akzeptieren	7/4A
to **add**	hinzufügen	7/2
addicted	abhängig	4/5
advantage	Vorteil	4/2
advice	Rat(schlag)	12/5HV
afraid	ängstlich	7/SD
Africa	Afrika	7/4A
album	Album	5/1
all night	die ganze Nacht	6/1
all over the world	auf der ganzen Welt	11/6HV
already	schon	9/1
American	Amerikaner/in	2/SB
anyone	(irgend)jemand	8/4HV
anyway	außerdem, überhaupt	4/SA
apartment	(US) Wohnung	9/5HV
to **appear**	Gast sein	5/1
to **apply**	sich bewerben	12/1
apprentice	Auszubildende/r, Lehrling	12/2A
apprenticeship	Berufsausbildung, Lehre	12/1
area	Gegend	9/1
argument	Streit	1/8A
armchair	Sessel	1/4A
to **arrange**	arrangieren, besorgen	10/6HV
artist	Künstler/in	9/S
as	da, weil	10/4
as … as	so … wie	7/4A
as an adult	als Erwachsener	11/1
at least	wenigstens	7/1A
at the back	hinten	9/S
at the front	vorne	9/S
atmosphere	Stimmung	2/1
to **attract**	anziehen	9/1
Australian	australisch	10/6
Austria	Österreich	10/S

B

badly treated	misshandelt	4/5
baggy	sehr weit	3/1
balcony	Balkon	1/3
to **be delighted**	sich freuen	10/6HV
to **be employed**	angestellt sein	12/1
to **be late**	zu spät kommen	4/1A
to **be worried**	sich Sorgen machen	4/5
to **become**	werden	4/1
Belfast	Stadt in Nordirland	5/1
Belgium	Belgien	10/S
to **believe**	glauben	8/4HV
best-known	bekannteste	8/S
between	zwischen	12/1
bill	Rechnung	11/7
blood	Blut	3/8
blouse	Bluse	3/2B
board	Tafel	11/6HV
to **book**	reservieren, buchen	10/5HV
boot	Stiefel	2/4A
born	geboren	5/1
boss	Chef	4/1
both	beide	4/1
bread roll	kleines weiches Brötchen	9/4
breadcrumbs	Paniermehl	7/2
breakdown	Panne	6/7HV
bridge	Brücke	9/S
brilliant	brillant, toll, genial	2/1
to **bring out**	herausbringen	5/1
Brit	Brite, Britin	8/1
Brit College for Performing Arts	Musik- und Schauspielschule in England	5/1
Britain	Großbritannien	5/1
brother-in-law	Schwager	1/2
to **brush**	bürsten	3/3A
bungee jumping	Bungeejumping	2/6B
Burma	Birma	5/1D
to **burst**	(herein)platzen	3/1
by bus	mit dem Bus	7/1A
by the way	übrigens	10/1

C

caller	Anrufer/in	11/4A
campsite	Zeltplatz	10/1
capital	Hauptstadt	10/SB
carpenter	Schreiner/in	12/5HV
carpet	Teppich	1/4A
carrot	Karotte	9/1D
to **carry out**	ausführen	11/1
cash desk	Kasse	11/3
cereal	Frühstücksgetreide	8/2
chance	Chance, Möglichkeit	12/1
to **change**	umsteigen	6/8
charity	wohltätiger Zweck	5/1
to **chat**	sich unterhalten	11/7
to **check the seasoning**	abschmecken	7/2
cheerful(ly)	fröhlich	8/2

chest of drawers	Kommode	1/4A
children's nurse	Kinderkranken-schwester	2/6A
to **choose**	aussuchen	2/4A
church	Kirche	9/6
cinema	Kino	2/1
to **climb**	klettern	AP/3
to **close**	schließen	11/8HV
clothes	Bekleidung	3/1
coffee table	Couchtisch	1/4A
colleague	Kollege, Kollegin	12/3
college	Berufs(fach)schule	3/1B
communication	Kommunikation	12/1
company	Firma	4/1
compost	Kompost	9/1
to **concentrate**	sich konzentrieren	4/2
consequence	Konsequenz, Folge	4/5C
to **contact**	Kontakt aufnehmen	11/6HV
continent	Kontinent	6/1
to **control**	kontrollieren, beherrschen	11/1
cooker	Herd	1/4A
cooking	Kochen	2/5A
costs	Kosten	8/4HV
course guide	Kursübersicht	12/5HV
cousin	Cousin, Cousine	1/2
cow	Kuh	9/6
crisps	(Kartoffel-)Chips	9/4
to **cross**	überqueren	10/4
crowded	voll (mit Menschen)	6/1
cucumber	Salatgurke	9/1
cupboard	Schrank	1/4A
curtain	Vorhang	1/4A
custom	Brauch	AP/3
customer	Kunde, Kundin	9/1
to **cut**	schneiden	3/8
cybercafe	Internet-Café	2/6B

D

dancing	Tanzen	2/5A
dangerous	gefährlich	9/1
dark	dunkel	2/4A
dealer	Händler/in, Dealer	9/1
Dear Sir	(Leserbrief) Anrede	11/7
to **decorate**	schmücken	AP/3
delay	Verspätung	6/7HV
delicious	lecker	6/1
to **deliver**	liefern	8/2
department	Abteilung	12/2B
to **describe**	beschreiben	3/1
diary	Tagebuch	8/2
difference	Unterschied	8/1
difficult	schwierig	2/1
difficulty	Schwierigkeit	10/4
direction	Richtung	6/7HV
dirty	schmutzig	9/1
disadvantage	Nachteil	4/2
to **discover**	entdecken	5/1
disk drive	Diskettenlaufwerk	11/S
DIY (Do It Yourself)	Heimwerker	8/2
double-decker	Doppeldecker	6/1
to **download**	herunterladen	11/7
downstairs	unten (im Haus)	1/4A
to **draw**	zeichnen	2/1
drawing	Zeichnung	2/1
driving licence	Führerschein	7/1A
driving test	Führerscheinprüfung	3/4
drug	Droge	4/5
during	während	2/1
DVD burner	DVD-Brenner	11/S
DVD drive	DVD-Laufwerk	11/S
DVD shop	DVD Verleih	5/2

E

to **earn**	verdienen	4/1
earring	Ohrring	3/7HV
east	östlich	8/S
egg	Ei	7/2
elective	Wahlfach	7/6HV
emergency number	Notruf	4/5
endless	endlos	1/8A
engine	Maschine, Motor	6/7HV
engineering	Technik; Maschinenbau	12/1
to **enjoy**	Spaß haben	2/1
enough	genug	6/4
Europe	Europa	8/S
even more	noch mehr	4/1
everybody	alle, jeder	3/1
exactly	genau	12/1
excellent	ausgezeichnet	8/1C
except	außer	9/6
exchange	Austausch	8/1
exciting	spannend, aufregend	2/6HV
expensive	teuer	10/1
experience	Erfahrung	12/5HV

F

factory	Fabrik	9/S
to **fall in love**	sich verlieben	4/3
family tree	Familien-Stammbaum	1/1D
fantastic	fantastisch	7/1A
far	weit (weg/entfernt)	1/1
fare	Fahrpreis	10/1B
farmer	Bauer, Farmer	1/1

fashion	Mode	3/SA
fast	schnell	4/1
favourite	liebste/r/s	10/2A
ferry	Fähre	6/7HV
to **fetch**	(ab)holen	8/4HV
field	Feld	1/1D
file	Datei	11/8HV
fishing	Fischerei	8/1
fishing	Angeln	10/3
to **fit**	passen	4/5HV
to **fix a time**	eine Zeit ausmachen	2/4A
flat	Wohnung	1/1
flat	flach	7/2
flea market	Flohmarkt	6/1
flight	Flug	6/7HV
for yourself	für dich (selbst)	4/SB
fork	Gabel	9/4
to **format**	formatieren	11/8HV
free	frei	8/4HV
fridge	Kühlschrank	1/4A
friendly	nett, freundlich	1/1
frustrated	frustriert	7/SD
full-time	Vollzeit	12/1
fun	Spaß	8/1
future	Zukunft	5/1

G

garage	Autowerkstatt	4/SA
gardener	Gärtner	2/1
gardening	Gartenarbeit	2/1
gentleman	Herr	10/6HV
Georgia	Georgien	5/1
German	deutsch	7/1A
Germany	Deutschland	7/1A
to **get caught**	erwischt werden	4/5HV
to **get married**	heiraten	4/3
to **get rid of**	loswerden	9/1
to **get there**	hinkommen	7/1A
to **give up (smoking)**	(das Rauchen) aufgeben	10/3
glad	froh	9/5HV
to **go sightseeing**	Sehenswürdigkeiten anschauen	6/1
to **go wrong**	schief gehen	4/2
grandparents	Großeltern	1/1
Great Britain	Großbritannien	8/S
great grandfather	Urgroßvater	1/2
great grandmother	Urgroßmutter	1/2
Greece	Griechenland	10/S
ground beef	Rinderhackfleisch	7/2
to **grow**	wachsen	9/1D
to **grow**	anpflanzen	9/6
to **grow up**	erwachsen werden	7/SB
guardian angel	Schutzengel	8/4HV
to **guess**	raten, schätzen	7/SHV
guide	Reiseführer	6/S
guitar	Gitarre	2/6B
guy	Typ	11/1

H

hairstylist	Frisörin	12/5HV
hall	Flur	1/SB
to **hang around**	herumhängen	11/7
to **happen**	passieren	4/2
hard	schwierig	2/1
hard	hart	4/1
hard disk	Festplatte	11/S
to **have (got) the nerve**	die Frechheit haben	7/SHV
to **have to**	müssen	3/1
he realized	es wurde ihm klar	11/1
headset	Headset	11/S
to **heat**	erhitzen	7/2
hill	Hügel	9/S
to **hit**	schlagen	2/1
hit	Hit	5/1
housewife	Hausfrau	1/1
huge	riesig	11/1
hundreds	Hunderte	7/4A
husband	Ehemann	8/4

I

important	wichtig	2/5A
to **impress**	beeindrucken	9/1
in addition	zusätzlich	12/1
in sight	in Sicht, zu sehen	3/1
in the late 1960s	Ende der 60er Jahre	11/1
in the middle	in der Mitte, mitten in	9/S
India	Indien	4/SA
Indian	indisch	7/1A
to **inform**	informieren	12/2A
inhabitant	Einwohner/in	10/6HV
to **install**	installieren, einsetzen	11/1
integrated modem	integriertes Modem	11/S
interested	interessiert	4/2
InterRail	InterRail (Zugreisen zu Sonderkonditionen)	10/1
invitation	Einladung	8/4
to **invite**	einladen	7/1C
Ireland	Irland	1/1
Israel	Israel	5/1D
It was real fun!	Es hat echt Spaß gemacht!	10/1

Italy	Italien	1/1

J

jewellery	Schmuck	3/1
joke	Witz	8/1
just now	jetzt gerade	3/5

K

keyboard	Tastatur	11/S
to **kick someone off**	jemanden rausschmeißen	4/5HV
kids	Kinder/junge Leute	1/1
kind	Art	5/S
knife, knives	Messer	9/4
known	bekannt	10/6HV

L

lady	Dame	10/6HV
lamp	(Steh-)Lampe	1/4A
language	Sprache	7/4A
large	groß	2/4A
(laser) printer	(Laser-)Drucker	11/S
to **last**	dauern	11/1
launderette	Waschsalon	AP/1
lb	Abkürzung für Pfund (453,6 g)	7/2
lead	Leine	9/2
to **leave**	verlassen	2/4A
leg	Bein	3/2B
to **lend**	leihen	6/4
level	Stufe	12/1
lift	Aufzug	6/S
to **load**	laden	11/8HV
local	aus der Gegend, örtlich	9/1
to **look at**	ansehen	3/3A
to **look like**	aussehen wie	3/1
lorry	LKW, Lastwagen	9/S
to **lose**	verlieren	4/1
lots of	viel(e)	1/1
loudspeaker	Lautsprecher	11/S
low	niedrig	6/1
luck	Glück	3/4
lunchtime	mittags	7/1A

M

magazine	Zeitschrift	2/1
main	Haupt-	9/3B
mainly	hauptsächlich	12/1
to **make fun of**	hänseln, aufziehen	3/4
to **make up one's mind**	sich entscheiden	11/7
match	Spiel	12/3
mate	Kumpel, Freund/in	2/5A
meal	Essen	7/1A
to **mean**	bedeuten	8/4B
means of transport	Verkehrsmittel	6/7B
mechanic	Mechaniker	1/1
media	Medien	5/S
to **meet**	(sich) treffen (mit)	2/4A
member	Mitglied	1/1D
midnight	Mitternacht	AP/1
mile	Meile (ca. 1,6 km)	6/4
milkman	Milchmann	8/2
to **miss**	vermissen	7/1A
to **mix**	vermischen	7/2
monitor	Bildschirm	11/S
most of all	am besten, am meisten	10/1
motor racing	Autorennen	8/1
mouse	Maus	11/S
to **move**	umziehen	5/1
move	(Spiel) Zug	11/1
to **move out**	aus-, wegziehen	9/1
Ms	Frau (auch für Unverheiratete)	3/1

N

nature	Natur	9/5HV
near	in der Nähe von	1/1
necessary	nötig	8/5
neighbour	Nachbar	2/1
nephew	Neffe	1/2
nervous	nervös	4/1
net	Netz	2/SB
newsagent's	Zeitungskiosk	5/2
next door	nebenan	1/1
next to	neben	5/2
niece	Nichte	1/2
noise	Lärm, Krach	9/3B
noisy	laut	9/3B
non-smoker	Nichtraucher/in	4/SB
non-smoking	Nichtraucher-	10/5HV
north	nördlich	8/S
northern	Nord-	8/S
not ... anything	nichts	4/1
not ... at all	überhaupt nicht	7/1A
not ... until	nicht ... vor	3/4
not ... yet	noch nicht	10/3
not even	noch nicht einmal	11/1
not the way	nicht so (wie)	1/8A

O

of course	natürlich	4/1
to **offer**	(an-)bieten	9/3B
older	älter	1/1
on time	pünktlich	4/1
one-day travelcard	Tagesfahrkarte	6/1

onion	Zwiebel	7/2A
on-the-job training	innerbetriebliche Ausbildung	12/1
orange juice	Orangensaft	9/4
order	Befehl	11/1
out of work	arbeitslos	1/1
outdoors	draußen	2/1
outside	draußen	2/1
over	vorbei	4/1
overalls	Overall	3/2B
overnight	über Nacht	10/5HV
to **own**	besitzen	5/2
own	eigene(r)	9/2
owner	Besitzer/in	5/2

P

to **pack**	(zusammen)packen	6/4
painless	schmerzlos	3/8
painter	Maler	4/1
paper-making	Papierherstellung	12/1
parking space	Parkplatz	3/1
to **pass**	vorbei fahren / gehen	10/6HV
passenger	Passagiere	6/7B
passport	Reisepass	7/5
peanut	Erdnuss	9/4
peanut butter cookie	Ernussbutterkeks	7/1A
per	pro	6/1
perfume	Parfüm	3/3A
personal style	persönlicher Stil	3/1
personnel manager	Personalchef/in	11/7
pet	Haustier	10/5HV
piercing	Piercing	3/8
pill	Tablette, Pille	4/5HV
plane	Flugzeug	9/S
plate	Teller	9/4
platform	Bahnsteig	10/5HV
pocket money	Taschengeld	6/1
to **pollute**	(Umwelt) verschmutzen	9/1
pony tail	zusammengebundene Haare (Zopf)	3/7HV
porcupine	Stachelschwein	7/2
port	Hafen	8/1
Portugal	Portugal	10/S
possibility	Möglichkeit	4/2
possible	möglich	7/4A
to **post**	abschicken	4/4A
pot	Topf	7/2
potato	Kartoffel	9/1D
practical	praktisch	4/1
practice	Übung; Training	7/6HV
to **prefer**	vorziehen	10/3
press release	Pressemitteilung	5/4
to **print**	drucken	11/1C
probably	wahrscheinlich	5/S
problem	Problem	3/1
to **produce**	produzieren	9/6
producer	Produzent	5/1
professional	professionell	3/8
project	Projekt	4/4B
pub	Kneipe	5/1D

Q

quarter	Schulsemester	7/6HV

R

racism	Rassismus	4/SB
railway	Bahnlinie	9/6
raw	ungekocht	7/2
really	wirklich	1/1
receptionist	Dame / Herr am Empfang	6/4
recipe	(Koch-)Rezept	7/2
record label	Plattenfirma	5/4
regular(ly)	regelmäßig	8/2
relaxed	locker	7/5
release	Neuerscheinung	5/4
to **release**	herausbringen	5/4
reporter	Reporterin	2/1
republic	Republik	8/S
required course	Pflichtfach	7/6HV
reservation	Reservierung	10/5HV
result	Ergebnis	11/1
revolution	Revolution	9/1
rice	Reis	7/2
ring	Ring	3/7HV
to **roll**	rollen	7/2
row	Reihe	5/2
rule	Regel	2/1
to **run a shop**	ein Geschäft leiten	11/5
to **run away**	weglaufen	4/5
rush hour	Hauptverkehrszeit	6/S
Russia	Russland	7/1A
Russian pancake	russischer Pfannkuchen	7/1A

S

sailing	Segeln	10/3
salad	(angemachter) Salat	9/4
sales	Vertrieb	12/2B
sales assistant	Verkäufer/in	11/3
salt	Salz	7/2
sauce	Soße	7/2
to **save**	sparen	9/5HV
to **save**	speichern	11/8HV
scanner	Bildabtaster, Scanner	11/S
school leaver	Schulabgänger/in	12/1
Scotland	Schottland	8/S

screen	Bildschirm	11/4A
seat	(Sitz-)Platz	10/5HV
second-hand	gebraucht	3/1
secretary	Sekretärin	3/1
See you then!	Bis dann!	3/5
to **send a text message**	eine SMS verschicken	2/3
shelf, shelves	Regal, Regale	1/4B
shop assistant	Verkäuferin	1/1
sick	krank	7/SB
sights	Sehenswürdigkeiten	10/4
silent	leise	11/1B
to **simmer**	köcheln	7/2
simple	einfach	9/5HV
sister-in-law	Schwägerin	1/2
to **sit down**	sich hinsetzen	2/4A
size	Größe	11/1
skill	Fähigkeit, Fertigkeit	11/7
skin	Haut	4/SA
skirt	Rock	3/2B
small ad	Kleinanzeige	2/SA
smell	Geruch	9/1
to **smile**	lächeln	4/2
snow	Schnee	6/7HV
soap	Seifenoper	5/7
So what?	Ja und?	7/1A
software program	Computerprogramm	11/1
some	einige	12/3
someone	jemand	3/1B
something	etwas	3/1B
sometimes	manchmal	2/1
soon	bald	4/1
Sounds good!	Hört sich gut an!	10/1
South	südlich	8/S
Spain	Spanien	10/S
Spanish	Spanisch	7/6HV
speed limit	Geschwindigkeits-begrenzung	8/4HV
to **speed up**	schneller machen	11/1
to **spend**	verbringen	2/1
to **spend**	ausgeben	11/6HV
spoon	Löffel	9/4
to **stand around**	herumstehen	3/1
to **staple**	tackern	3/8
star	Star	5/1
to **stay alone**	allein bleiben	2/4A
to **steal**	stehlen	4/5
still	(immer) noch	3/4
stop and go traffic	stockender Verkehr	6/S
storey	Etage	1/4C
to **stretch out**	sich ausgestreckt hinlegen	1/6HV
student	Schüler/in	3/1
style	Stil	3/SA
subject	Fach	7/6HV
successful	erfolgreich	5/1
such a	solch ein/e/r	10/4
to **surf**	surfen	7/6HV
swimming	Schwimmen	4/3C
to **switch off**	ausschalten	11/8HV
to **switch on**	einschalten	5/3
Switzerland	die Schweiz	10/S

T

to **take a test**	eine Prüfung machen	3/4
tattoo	Tätowierung	3/8
teaspoon	Teelöffel	7/2
ten years ago	vor 10 Jahren	1/1
terrible	schrecklich	4/5
to **test**	testen	3/3A
Thanks a lot!	Vielen Dank!	4/4B
the Netherlands	die Niederlande	10/S
thin	dünn	1/8A
thought	Gedanke	6/1
through	durch	5/1
tic-tac-toe	Spiel	11/1
to **tidy up**	aufräumen	3/5
tie	Schlips, Krawatte	3/2B
tight	eng	3/1
tights	Strumpfhose	3/2B
tired	müde	4/1
tonight	heute Abend	7/1A
tour	Tournee	5/4
towards	auf ... zu	12/1
traffic	Verkehr	10/4
traffic lights	Verkehrsampel	9/S
to **train**	ausgebildet werden	4/1
trainer	Ausbilder/in	12/2B
trendsetter	Trendsetter	8/1
trouble	Ärger, Probleme	4/1
trousers	Hose	3/2B
to **try on**	anprobieren	3/3A
Turkey	Türkei	7/5
Turkish	türkisch	7/1A
to **turn red**	rot werden	7/SHV
to **type in**	eintippen	11/1
typical	typisch	8/5

U

umbrella	Regenschirm	3/4
unemployed	arbeitslos	11/7
unhappy	unglücklich	4/5
United Kingdom (UK)	Vereinigtes Königreich	8/S
university	Universität	4/1
unpaid	unbezahlt	2/6B
upstairs	oben (im Haus)	1/4A
USB port	USB-Port	11/S

useful	nützlich	10/4
usually	normalerweise	2/4A

V

vegetable	Gemüse	9/1
vegetarian	vegetarisch	6/1
village	Dorf	2/1
violent	gewalttätig	5/5
vocational	Berufs-, beruflich	8/1

W

to **wait**	warten	6/4
waitress	Bedienung	3/2A
to **wake someone up**	jemanden wecken	4/2
Wales	Wales	8/S
wardrobe	Kleiderschrank	1/4A
washbasin	Waschbecken	1/4C
watch	(Armband-)Uhr	3/2B
wax model	Wachsfigur	6/1
to **wear**	(Kleidung) tragen	3/SB
weather	Wetter	10/1
web site	Webseite	7/6HV
webcam	Webcam	11/S
west	westlich	8/S
What about …?	Was ist mit …?	3/1
What kind of …?	Was für …?	3/7HV
What's on?	Was läuft?	2/4A
whatever	was auch immer	5/1
while	während	10/6HV
whistle	Pfeife; Anpfiff	2/4A
window	Fenster	1/4A
wish	Wunsch	2/6A
to **wish**	wünschen	3/4
without	ohne	4/SA
world	Welt	7/4A
world-class	Weltklasse	8/1
worried	besorgt	7/SD

Y

YHA	Jugendherbergs-vereinigung	6/1
youth hostel	Jugendherberge	6/1

Quellenverzeichnis

Titel: Avenue Images GmbH (IT Stock Free RF), Hamburg • S. 5: Getty Images PhotoDisc (PhotoDisc), Hamburg; Sharp Electronics Europe, Hamburg; iStockphoto (Jostein Hauge), Calgary, Alberta; Höllerer, Conrad, Stuttgart; iStockphoto (Good Creative), Calgary, Alberta; MEV, Augsburg; Philips GmbH, Hamburg; iStockphoto (Cristina Fumi), Calgary, Alberta; Ingram Publishing, Tattenhall Chester • S. 6: Avenue Images GmbH (Image Source RF), Hamburg; Bananastock RF, Watlington / Oxon • S. 8: ALNO AG, Pfullendorf; iStockphoto (Tyler), Calgary, Alberta; Flötotto Einrichtungssysteme, Gütersloh • S. 10: Klett-Archiv (Katja Schüch), Stuttgart; Corel Corporation, Unterschleissheim • S. 14: BMW AG, München; Avenue Images GmbH (Image Source RF), Hamburg; Avenue Images GmbH (Image Source), Hamburg; Avenue Images GmbH (image 100), Hamburg; Fotosearch RF, Waukesha, WI; MEV, Augsburg • S. 16: Avenue Images GmbH (Image Source), Hamburg • S. 17: Avenue Images GmbH (Rubberball RF), Hamburg; Bananastock RF, Watlington / Oxon; Avenue Images GmbH (Image Source / RF), Hamburg; Bananastock RF, Watlington / Oxon; Imageshop RF, Düsseldorf • S. 18: Bananastock RF, Watlington / Oxon • S. 23: Das Fotoarchiv, Essen • S. 25: Das Fotoarchiv, Essen • S. 26: Image Source (RF), Köln • S. 29: Alamy Images RM (Nordicphotos), Abingdon, Oxon; iStockphoto (Christian Weber), Calgary, Alberta; Fotosearch RF (Brand X Pictures), Waukesha, WI • S. 30: ullstein bild (Malzkorn), Berlin; ullstein bild (Brinckmann), Berlin; Corel Corporation, Unterschleissheim; JupiterImages (RF/photos.com), Tucson, AZ; iStockphoto (Mats Lund), Calgary, Alberta • S. 35: MEV, Augsburg; Corel Corporation, Unterschleissheim; Getty Images (Photodisc), München; Mel Smith Photography, Nottingham • S. 37: Image 100 (RF), Berlin; ullstein bild (Röhrbein), Berlin; Alamy Images RM (Alan Copson), Abingdon, Oxon; Getty Images RF (PhotoDisc), München • S. 38: Corel Corporation, Unterschleissheim; Fotosearch RF (Brand X Pictures), Waukesha, WI • S. 41: iStockphoto (RF/Fleuren), Calgary, Alberta; iStockphoto (RF/Neudert), Calgary, Alberta; Avenue Images GmbH (RF/ Stockbyte), Hamburg • S. 42: Avenue Images GmbH (Stockbyte), Hamburg; Das Fotoarchiv (RF), Essen • S. 43: iStockphoto (RF/Ledray), Calgary, Alberta; iStockphoto (RF/Tan), Calgary, Alberta; iStockphoto (RF/Skelton), Calgary, Alberta • S. 48: iStockphoto (RF), Calgary, Alberta; Fotosearch RF (RF), Waukesha, WI; Corel Corporation, Unterschleissheim • S. 52: Getty Images (Photodisc), München; iStockphoto (RF/ Ling), Calgary, Alberta; MEV, Augsburg; iStockphoto (RF/ Wadowski), Calgary, Alberta • S. 54: iStockphoto (RF/Lorenzo), Calgary, Alberta • S. 57: iStockphoto (RF/Lobo), Calgary, Alberta; iStockphoto (RF/Johnson), Calgary, Alberta • S. 59: Alamy Images RM (RF), Abingdon, Oxon • S. 60: Getty Images (Taxi/Murray), München • S. 64: iStockphoto (RF/ Derics), Calgary, Alberta; Creativ Collection Verlag GmbH, Freiburg; MEV, Augsburg • S. 65: obs (Creativelabs), Hamburg; obs (Dell), Hamburg; Epson Deutschland GmbH, Meerbusch; iStockphoto (RF), Calgary, Alberta • S. 66: Corbis (Doug Wilson), Düsseldorf • S. 71: iStockphoto (RF), Calgary, Alberta; Getty Images PhotoDisc, Hamburg; Getty Images, München; Avenue Images GmbH (Image Source), Hamburg; Avenue Images GmbH (Brand X Pictures), Hamburg; Corbis (Bob Rowan; Progressi), Düsseldorf • S. 72: Bananastock RF, Watlington / Oxon; Verband deutscher Papierfabriken e., Bonn • S. 76: ullstein bild (Rufenach), Berlin; Getty Images (taxi/silver), München; Getty Images (Photodisc), München • S. 77: MEV, Augsburg; Fotosearch RF (Digital Vision), Waukesha, WI; Bananastock RF, Watlington / Oxon; PhotoDisc, Seattle, WA • S. 119, 120: Klett-Archiv • Activity pages: Fotosearch RF (Brand X Pictures), Waukesha, WI; iStockphoto (RF), Calgary, Alberta; iStockphoto (RF/ Cowan), Calgary, Alberta; iStockphoto (RF/ Burka), Calgary, Alberta; iStockphoto (RF/ Wodzicki), Calgary, Alberta; iStockphoto (RF/ Dowling), Calgary, Alberta

Hörverständnistexte

Die hier nicht aufgeführten Texte der CD sind bereits im vorderen Teil des Buches in den Units abgedruckt. Für Unit 7 (Starter Seite) wurde ein Rap aufgenommen.

Unit 1 Listening, 6

Sally: At last I've got my own room! My brother has got a flat now and so I've got his room. I can't tell you how happy I am – and my parents say I can do what I like with my room. First I want to paint the walls – blue or green, they say soft colours help you relax. So when I get home, I can shut the door, stretch out on the bed and relax. And then, there's my music: I can listen to it day and night – that's really cool! I can put the CD player near the bed and my CDs on the shelves on the wall. And if I want I can have my friends there and we can talk and listen to music and do lots of other things. That's great and I'm really happy!

Unit 2 Listening, 6

Max: Well, my name's Max and I finish school this year. I'm lucky, I've got a job as a car mechanic. I start in September. I spend a lot of my free time with my computer. I usually play games on it. But I would really like to go out and meet more people.

Liz: Hi, I'm Liz. I work as a shop assistant in a supermarket. The job is not very interesting. I watch a lot of TV and I like music. But I would really like to do something different and exciting.

Ann: I'm Ann. I haven't got a job at the moment. I would really like to be a children's nurse but I need to get some more qualifications first. I read a lot of books and magazines but I get bored with that.

Unit 3 Listening, 7

Interviewer: Hello, I'm from "Style and Modern Living" magazine. I'm writing about young people, their style and fashion and what they like. Can I ask you and your girlfriend a few questions?

Tim: Yeah, why not? What do you want to know?

Interviewer: Well, here's the first question. I see you're wearing jewellery. What kind of jewellery do you like?

Ann: I love all kinds of jewellery. Today I'm wearing three small earrings. I also like rings.

Interviewer: What other jewellery are you wearing today?

Ann: I'm wearing a ring, but only one. Sometimes I wear two or three. My boyfriend Tim isn't wearing any jewellery. He thinks that's only for girls.

Interviewer: Tim, can you tell me: What is 'style' for you?

Tim: Hmm, style is … not always to be like other people. I have a pony tail because I don't want to look like Joe Bloggs or people like that.

Interviewer: Yeah. What else does style mean to you?

Tim: Style's also about the colours you wear. Ann and I are wearing black today; we love the colour black. It always looks really good.

Interviewer: Is music important to you?

Tim: Not very.

Interviewer: Okay, that's all. Thanks very much.

Unit 4 Listening, 5

Lori: Hi! My name's Lori. I'm seventeen. I'm okay now, but two years ago I had some trouble. I felt bad because I didn't have a boyfriend. So I started to eat too much. I ate and ate and ate. I spent all my money on chocolate. Then my clothes didn't fit – they were much too tight. I talked to my mom. She told me that lots of people have to wait before they can find the right boyfriend or girlfriend.

Chris: I'm Chris. I was on the best football team in the city. But the trainer kicked me off the team. We had a really important game and I didn't feel very well. I was so tired: I was at the disco until late. I just took one little pill to play better. But the trainer saw me and I got caught. I'm sixteen, and I hope I can play again next year.

Unit 5 Listening, 6

Jeff: Hi Liz. Are you okay?

Liz: Yeah, but I'm a bit tired. I did some shopping after work. – You're late. What happened?

Jeff: Well, I called in at the DVD shop to get a DVD for this evening, but…

Liz: You mean we've got nothing to watch?! What are we going to do?

Jeff: No problem. I bought a newspaper at the newsagent's, so we can find out what's on TV.

Liz: Oh great! You know there's never anything good on a Saturday evening. Oh well, come on – show me the paper.

Jeff: Here look! On BBC 1 – comedy – 'Mr Bean'. That's at 6.30. You know how funny that is.

Liz: Hmm, too late! It's six o' clock now and we have to eat something first. But look, there's another comedy at 6.45 on BBC 2 'Have I got news for you!'

Jeff: So we're going to watch that then, are we? Aren't there any films on?

Liz: Sure. On BBC 2 there's 'A night to remember'. That's at 7.45. On BBC 1 at 9 o' clock 'Mario and the Boss' – oh that's a crime story, I don't like them. Hmm, look, on Channel 4, a romantic comedy at 8.30, 'What happened last night?' – that sounds good.

Jeff: Does it? I hate romantic films. I want to watch a thriller or a detective series – something with a bit of action.

Liz: Well, on ITV at 8 there's 'The Bill'. I like that, too. Then we could watch a documentary programme on ITV at 8.30. It's about rich people.

Jeff: Yeah. Not bad really, for a Saturday evening. Okay, let's do the cooking, I'm hungry.

Unit 6 Listening, 7

1. NorthSea Ferries are pleased to inform passengers that the 18.00 Dover / Calais ferry is ready to leave. The engine has now been repaired.
2. King's Cross Station. Due to an accident, the 10.25 train to Aberdeen is 15 minutes late.
3. Flight BA 486 from Gatwick to Dublin. Would all passengers please go to Gate 3? We are sorry for the delay which was due to heavy snow at Dublin Airport.
4. Green Park. Green Park. Passengers for Heathrow Airport please change to Piccadilly Line. The train will be 10 minutes late because of a breakdown.

Unit 7 Listening, 6

1. elective	4. Spanish	7. quarter
2. website	5. surf	8. required
3. practice	6. subject	9. cheerleading

Unit 8 Listening, 4

Lucy: Jamie is going to be eighteen on Thursday. What does he want for his birthday?

Will: I think he wants money for his driving licence.

Lucy: Well, the first thing all kids think about is a driving licence! They really think that they are grown up. When they can drive, they think they are free.

Will: Yeah, it's not as easy as that.

Lucy: Many kids believe that they don't have to listen to anyone when they are eighteen. I've seen so many accidents with nice kids who don't believe that speed limits were made for them. Speed means everything to some of them.

Will: Well, most of the time there's a guardian angel that helps them.

Lucy: But sometimes the guardian angels aren't there. – And then there are the costs. Some parents and grandparents pay for everything – the licence, the car – everything. I ask myself if that is good for the kids. But you know, sometimes parents are just happy that they don't have to drive to the disco at two in the morning to fetch their children. I would worry.

Will: Yes, but you worry about everything.

Lucy: I worry that Jamie will drink and drive.

Will: He won't do that. Jamie's a good kid. The good thing is that he can drive with his parents until he takes the driving test. He just needs the large red 'L' on the car, like all learners.

Lucy: Mmmh.

Unit 9 Listening, 5

Ron: I'm Ron and I live here in Maine, USA. I moved here with my parents last year. We lived in Chicago before that. I was glad to move. Chicago is a big, dangerous city – there's a lot of street crime. Anyway, then my pa lost his job, but he had saved some money and so he bought this farm. I'm glad he did – it's a great life here. I help him on the farm – you know, driving the tractor and so on. I even have two dogs which I love. In Chicago, we couldn't have dogs, our apartment was too small. I guess my parents want to live a really simple life here, so we don't have a TV or a telephone. We try to save as much energy as possible – next year we're going to use energy from the wind or the sun. Life is really great here, but I sometimes miss some of my friends in Chicago.

Patty: I met my boyfriend Paul on a training course in New York two years ago. Well, when we'd finished the course he said to me: 'Patty', (that's my name), 'I've had enough of the city,' (he's always been a real nature freak) – 'let's go out west'. Well, we had nothing to lose so we came out here to live together in a small town in California. We both got jobs in the fruit industry and I can't tell you how great it is out here. The weather is so much better and the people are friendlier. Small towns are much cleaner and quieter, too. We don't have a lot of money of course – we'd have more in New York, but we do have a better life. The only thing I sometimes miss is seeing the latest movies in the movie theater.

Unit 10 Listening, 6

Tourist guide in Rome:

Good afternoon, ladies and gentlemen. I'm delighted to show you around our beautiful city of Rome, capital of Italy. Rome is more than two thousand years old and almost three million people live here.
Our first stop will be the famous Colosseum which I think is also known in your country. We'll have twenty minutes to look around. After that we'll be going to the Forum Romanum, where … If you don't have any plans for tonight, go to the Piazza Navona and enjoy a nice evening out; you can …

Tourist guide in Berlin:

Welcome to Happy Tours. We're now starting our two-hour tour of Berlin, which became the capital of Germany again in 1990. About three and a half million people live here. We're passing the Reichstagsgebäude at the moment … and over there you can see the famous Brandenburger Tor which was built around 1790. By the way, while we're waiting at the traffic lights we can talk about what you can do tonight. There's a new musical on called "The Good Life". I could arrange tickets for you …

Tourist guide in Barcelona:

Good afternoon, everybody. Welcome to Barcelona, the second biggest city in Spain with nearly two million inhabitants. Madrid, which is the capital, is the biggest city with more than three million inhabitants. Right now we're passing the Casa Milá, one of those interesting houses by the architect Antoni Gaudi. … Another famous sight is the Picasso museum which you can visit tomorrow morning. Tonight it is possible to see a flamenco show at the concert hall near your hotel. … Our bus is turning left now and right in front of you is …

Unit 11 Listening, 8

Speaker: Please listen and go on step by step. You can ask me, of course, if you have any questions. First of all we all turn on our computers. Then we must load our word processing program. All right? We are going to write a new text, so we must open a new file. Okay? Now type your letter to "The Evening Post". This will take some minutes, of course. – When you have finished you should give the letter the right form, that means that you have to format the text. Then make a printout of your letter and see if it looks okay. Don't forget to save your text at the end because you may need it again. – Everything all right? – Good. Close your file, leave the program and finally switch off the computer. That's all for now. But don't forget to post your letter today! …

Unit 12 Listening, 5

Matthew: Hi, I'm Matthew. … I'm 19 and in my second year of NVQ in Business Studies at Kent College. When I left school I thought I wanted to work as a car mechanic. After a year I found that I had made a mistake and that I would prefer to work in a shop. College informed me that I had the chance to change. So I started a course as a shop assistant more than a year ago. I hope to finish college next year and get a good job then.

Helen: Hello, my name's Helen. I'm 17 years old. I'm studying for an NVQ in Hairstyling. I'm in my first year. You see, I've got a friend who did this course two years ago. She's a hairstylist now and she likes it very much. So I decided to go to Hartford College one day a week, and the rest of the time I spend with an employer to get work experience. I am learning, working, and getting money for it.

Sarah: I'm Sarah. I've just had my 16th birthday. I'm taking the first year of a two-year NVQ in Carpentry at Stanford College. I've always felt I wanted to do something unusual. My grandfather was a carpenter, and when I looked at the college course guide I knew it was for me. Our college is great. I'm really enjoying my course and I've made lots of friends. My advice to everybody is: Go to college and get your qualifications!

Activity page 2

Colin comes home from work one evening.

Colin Angie, where are you? Look, I've got our honeymoon photos.

Angie Oh, hello Colin. Let's look at them. Oh, it's Canterbury where we started. Canterbury was such a nice old town. Canterbury Cathedral was so beautiful inside. I was surprised that you could buy such beautiful old things as well as modern and expensive clothes in Canterbury.

Colin Yes, that was the beginning of the "shopping tour". I think you went shopping in all of the towns we visited.

Angie That's right. I bought things to remember our fantastic holiday.

Colin Well okay. Here's a photo of Tower Bridge in London. And there you are in front of Buckingham Palace.

Angie We were real tourists in London: Do you remember? We had lunch at Covent Garden, the old vegetable and fruit market, and listened to the musicians there. And we relaxed in Hyde Park and we went shopping in Harrods and Liberty's.

Colin One day we must visit London again.

Angie Oh, yes please.

Colin Then we travelled south to Hever Castle. Look here's a photo of Hever Castle. Wasn't Henry VIII's wife Anne Boleyn born there?

Angie Yes, she was. The gardens there were beautiful.

Colin Oh, Angie, look. Here we are in Brighton. We watched the sea for hours.

Angie Oh yes, and we had dinner on Brighton Pier. Fish and chips, hmm.

Colin Yes and we went to the funfair on the pier.

Angie You liked that! The next day we travelled west to Stonehenge. I can't imagine how the stones were put there 5,000 years ago. The people didn't have any machines then.

Colin You're right. It was amazing. Look here's a photo of Torquay in Devon. That's south-west of Stonehenge. We wore our summer clothes because it was as sunny as in Italy. It even looked like Italy with the plants and trees.

Angie Oh, it was so romantic. And we ate scones with clotted cream and jam. I couldn't eat anything for supper because I had eaten too many.

Colin And the next day we drove north past Bristol. We stopped in Stratford-upon-Avon where William Shakespeare, the famous writer, was born. We visited his home there, too.

Angie Why didn't we stay longer? It looked so beautiful.

Colin We had already spent too much time in the south. We wanted to go around England, you know.

Angie Yes, but when we arrived in Birmingham we forgot our plans. We saw the sign for the "Black Country Living Museum" in Dudley and we spent a day there.

Colin The open air museum was great. I loved the old-fashioned school and the electric tramcars and the old shops. Do you remember the breadman with the basket of bread? Here he is with his horse.

Angie It was very interesting.

Colin The next day wasn't interesting. We drove all of the way north to Nottingham. That's north-east of Birmingham. I loved Sherwood Forest.

Angie Yes, I loved it, too. When I was a child, I read lots of stories about Robin Hood and how he stole money from the rich and gave it to the poor people.

Colin So did I.

Angie I was sad when we didn't stop in Liverpool.

Colin I know but we wanted to get to the Lake District. It was time to relax and do nothing.

Angie Do nothing? You call swimming, a boat trip, water-skiing, cycling and mountain-climbing nothing?

Colin Well, no but it was fun. That day we walked to the waterfall was great.

Angie Yeah. The last two days in York were relaxing. We stayed in a fantastic hotel. I felt like a queen.

Colin I liked the Shambles in York with the narrow streets, and old houses and shops. I drank tea while you went shopping. Didn't you buy those jeans in York?

Angie Yes, and the red pullover with the flowers.

Colin After your shopping trip we walked round the town.

Angie Yes, it was beautiful. But that night we didn't feel as happy. Do you remember?

Colin Oh yes, I do. We went on a "Ghost Walk". The guide told us ghost stories about York.

Angie He did a good job. The trip was wonderful. I'd like to go back to York next year.

Colin That's a good idea! We can start in York and then visit some other interesting places.

Orkney Islands
Outer Hebrides
ATLANTIC OCEAN
North Sea
Inverness
Loch Ness
Aberdeen
Ben Nevis
Tay
Scotland
Edinburgh
Glasgow
Clyde
Londonderry
Northern Ireland
Belfast
Newcastle
Carlisle
Tyne
GREAT BRITAIN
Keswick
Lake District
Cumbria
Windermere
Kendal
Isle of Man
Yorkshire
Connemara
Harrogate
York
Irish Sea
Blackpool
Preston
Hull
REPUBLIC OF IRELAND
Dublin
Manchester
Leeds
Liverpool
Shannon
Holyhead
Llanfair P. G.
Llandudno
Snowdon
Sheffield
England
Limerick
Nottingham
Leicester
Peterborough
Waterford
Rosslare
Dunmore East
Birmingham
Coventry
Wales
Solihull
Severn
Fishguard
Stratford-upon-Avon
Cambridge
Ipswich
Tredegar
Gloucester
Colchester
Harwich
Swansea
Bladon
Oxford
Headington
London
Cardiff
Thames
Bristol
Bath
Windsor
Gravesend
Canterbury
Kent
Dover
Folkestone
Somerset
Salisbury
Southampton
Exeter
Bournemouth
Portsmouth
Brighton
Eastbourne
Devon
Exmouth
Cowes
Isle of Wight
Weymouth
Cornwall
Torquay
Plymouth
English Channel
Land's End
Channel Islands

U.S.S.R.
ARCTIC OCEAN
Bering Str.
Queen Elizabeth Islands
GREENLAND
ICELAND
Baffin Bay
Baffin Island
Victoria I.
Alaska
Yukon
Anchorage
Whitehorse
Juneau
Mackenzie
North West Territories
Rocky Mountains
Brit. Columbia
Alberta
Edmonton
Saskatchewan
Manitoba
Nelson
Hudson Bay
Labrador
Newfoundland
St. John's
Quebec
Ontario
Calgary
Regina
Winnipeg
Victoria
Seattle
Washington
PACIFIC OCEAN
Lake Superior
The Great Lakes
Ottawa
Quebec
New Brunswick
Fredericton
St. Lawrence
Halifax
Nova Scotia
Maine
Montana
North Dakota
Minnesota
Oregon
Boise
Idaho
Yellowstone Nat. Park
South Dakota
Wyoming
Wisconsin
Lake Michigan
Michigan
Lake Huron
Toronto
Lake Ontario
VT
NH
MA
Boston
CT
RI
NY
New York
Detroit
L. Erie
PA
Pittsburgh
NJ
East Orange
Philadelphia
DE
Washington D.C.
Sierra Nevada
Nevada
Utah
Nebraska
Iowa
Chicago
Ohio
Columbus
Dayton
Indiana
Illinois
Indianapolis
Missouri
Mississippi
San Francisco
Fresno
California
Colorado
Denver
Kansas
St. Louis
Ohio
KY
WV
VA
Appalachian Mts.
ATLANTIC OCEAN
Las Vegas
Grand Canyon
Mojave Desert
Painted Desert
Pawhuska
Tulsa
Nashville
TN
NC
Los Angeles
Barstow
Flagstaff
Albuquerque
Amarillo
Oklahoma
Oklahoma City
Lawton
Arkansas
Birmingham
SC
Oceanside
Phoenix
Arizona
New Mexico
The Great Plains
Alabama
Georgia
MS
Dallas
Texas
Lower California
Rio Grande
Houston
LA
New Orleans
Florida
Miami
BAHAMAS
Gulf of Mexico
Havana
CUBA
MEXICO
Mexico City
0
1000 km
0
1000 Miles
CT Connecticut
DE Delaware
KY Kentucky
LA Louisiana
MA Massachusetts
MS Mississippi
NC North Carolina
NH New Hampshire
NJ New Jersey
NY New York
PA Pennsylvania
RI Rhode Island
SC South Carolina
TN Tennessee
VA Virginia
VT Vermont
WV West Virginia